Rough Men, Tough Men

OTHER BOOKS BY WILLIAM COLE

A Book of Love Poems
Oh, What Nonsense!
D. H. Lawrence: Poems Selected for Young People
The Sea, Ships and Sailors
A Book of Nature Poems

Rough Men, Tough Men

Poems of Action and Adventure

Edited by WILLIAM COLE

Illustrated by Enrico Arno

The Viking Press   *New York*

ACKNOWLEDGMENTS

Acknowledgment is made to the following publishers and authors or their representatives for their permission to use copyright material. Every reasonable effort has been made to clear the use of the poems in this volume with the copyright owners. If notified of any omissions the editor and publisher will gladly make the proper corrections in future editions.

Allans Music (Australia) Pty. Ltd., Melbourne, for "The Swagless Swaggie" by Edward Harrington.

Angus & Robertson Ltd., Sydney, for "The Dead Swagman" from *The Dancing Bough* by Nancy Cato.

Atheneum Publishers, for "On a Portrait by Copley" from the book *Apollonian Poems* by Arthur Freeman, copyright © 1961 by Arthur Freeman. Reprinted by permission of Atheneum Publishers.

John Blight, for his poem "Camp Fever," reprinted by permission of Hutchinson and Company, London, and John Blight.

Brandt & Brandt, for "The Sack of Old Panama" from *Poems* by Dana Burnet, copyright 1943 by Dana Burnet.

Collins-Knowlton-Wing, Inc., for "Sergeant-Major Money" and "1805" by Robert Graves, copyright 1955 by Robert Graves. Both reprinted by permission of Collins-Knowlton-Wing, Inc.

Coward-McCann, for "Chicago Idyll" by E. Merrill Root, reprinted by permission of Coward-McCann, Inc., from *Lyric America: An Anthology of American Poetry*, edited by Alfred Kreymborg. Copyright 1930, 1941, 1958 by Alfred Kreymborg.

Dodd, Mead & Company, for "My Friends" and "The Shooting of Dan McGrew," reprinted by permission of Dodd, Mead & Company, Inc., from *The Collected Poems of Robert Service*.

Doubleday & Co., Inc., for "Bill 'Awkins," "Danny Deever," "Harp Song of the Dane Women," and "The Lament of the Border Cattle Thief" from the book *Rudyard Kipling's Verse*, reprinted by permission of Mrs. George Bambridge and Doubleday & Company, Inc.

Faber and Faber Ltd., Publishers, for "Conquerors" from *The Haunted Garden* by Henry Treece.

Mrs. Hazel Fetzer, for "The Dick Johnson Reel" from *The Bulls of Spring* by Jake Falstaff, copyright 1937 by G. P. Putnam's Sons, Inc., renewed 1965 by Mrs. Hazel Fetzer.

David Higham Associates, Ltd., for "Ballad of the Long Drop" from *Collected Poems* by John Pudney, and for "Cowboy Song" from *Union Street* by Charles Causley.

Holt, Rinehart & Winston, Inc., for "The Ballad of William Sycamore" from *Ballads and Poems* by Stephen Vincent Benét, copyright 1931 by Stephen Vincent Benét, copyright © 1959 by Rosemary Carr Benét. Reprinted by permission of Holt, Rinehart & Winston, Inc.

Houghton Mifflin Company, for "Charley Lee" from *Songs of the Lost Frontier* by Henry Herbert Knibbs, copyright 1930 by Henry H. Knibbs, copyright © renewed 1958, and for "The Wolves" from *What a Kingdom It Was* by Galway Kinnell, copyright © 1960 by Galway Kinnell. Both reprinted by permission of the publisher, Houghton Mifflin Company.

Page 256 constitutes an extension of this copyright page.

Contents

Introduction 7

Away Out West 11

Sea Dogs and Buccaneers 39

Knights and Deeds 69

Killers 85

The Fighting Irish 109

In Faraway Places 127

Robbers and Outlaws 157

Brawlers 177

The Blast of War 197

Independent Spirits 223

Index of Authors 246

Index of Titles 251

Introduction

If you can't stand the sight of the word blood, this book is not for you. These are poems of adventure, mostly on frontiers where "men are men, and women are glad of it," and a certain amount of gore spills over the pages.

The phrase "rough men, tough men" doesn't necessarily mean men who get into fights; some of the toughest men in the world have never in their adult lives exchanged a hard fist with a fellow man. Good men are rough and tough in a variety of ways: in their independent spirits; in their adventurousness; in their readiness to speak up against injustice. Men as varied as Dr. Spock and the astronauts, as John Kennedy and Floyd Patterson, come under my definition of rough and tough. You will note that there are very few poems that celebrate war—war is not anything to celebrate—and quite a few that are definitely antiwar, such as the powerful "Dooley Is a Traitor," which is about a *really* tough guy who doesn't see why he should become part of an army. There are very few intelligent men who have had a fist fight after the age of sixteen. Excepting professional boxers, of course. Speaking of which, one of the best poets in this collection, Vernon Scannell, *was* a professional boxer (and looks it), before he took up the somewhat more delicate craft of poet.

About half of these poets, including Mr. Scannell, are English. Two of the most authentic-sounding cowboy ballads are by contemporary Englishmen who have probably never even been within smelling distance of a genuine cowboy. An interesting difference between the English and the American approaches can be seen in the ballads about the American outlaw, Samuel Hall, and his English counterpart, Jack Hall. Note how much less polite the American is, cursing "Damn your eyes!" at everyone.

There are an awful lot of Irish in here, too. I've often wondered why the Irish have such a reputation for fighting. Surely the Latin races are more quick-tempered? There haven't been many first-rate Irish boxers. (The only Irish boxer I ever heard of had the nickname "Canvasback Doyle," indicating that he was more frequently horizontal than vertical in the ring.) Perhaps the Irish reputation for fighting stems from the fact that so many Irish were forced to leave their country during the famine in the eighteen-forties and, in order to survive, opened up frontiers or fought in other people's armies. Or it could be that, as a nation, they fought against England so hard and so long that the name of "the fighting race" hung on. Their reputation in America comes partly from the name given the aggressive Notre Dame football team—"The Fighting Irish." The fact that most of the members of the team have always been Polish has done nothing to lessen the impact—they've probably never even considered changing their name to "The Fighting Polish."

There's a lot of miscellaneous geographical and historical information in these poems. I even picked up a tip on proper pronunciation; in Robert Graves' poem about Lord Nelson, "1805," it is obvious from the meter that the name of the place where Nelson's famous sea battle occurred is pronounced Traffle-gar, not, as we have always believed, Trafálgar. You might have to wait years for the opportunity to work that into a conversation, but it will be worth it.

Obviously, the toughest men will be found where life is toughest—on the frontiers: the rugged sheep country of Australia, the gold-mining settlements of Alaska, and our own Wild West. But that was all some time ago, and by now we've pretty much run out of frontiers; there's no place left on this earth for men to go adventuring, so there isn't much of this kind of adventure poetry being written. This is saddening . . . but wait! How about—some years hence—a sequel about rough men and tough men on Pluto, on Jupiter! What worlds of poetry lie ahead!

William Cole

AWAY OUT WEST

Whisky Bill

A-down the road and gun in hand
Comes Whisky Bill, mad Whisky Bill;
A-lookin' for some place to land
Comes Whisky Bill.
An' everybody'd like to be
Ten miles away behind a tree
When on his joyous, aching spree
Starts Whisky Bill.

The times have changed since you made love,
O Whisky Bill, O Whisky Bill!
The happy sun grinned up above
At Whisky Bill.
And down the middle of the street
The sheriff comes on toe and feet
A-wishin' for one fretful peek
At Whisky Bill.

The cows go grazing o'er the lea—
Poor Whisky Bill! Poor Whisky Bill!
An' aching thoughts pour in on me
Of Whisky Bill.
The sheriff up and found his stride;
Bill's soul went shootin' down the slide—
How are things on the Great Divide,
O Whisky Bill?

American cowboy ballad

The Dick Johnson Reel

*(The old men say their grandfathers heard Dick Johnson
sing the chorus of this song in the timberlands of northern
Summit County, Ohio.)*

Old Dick Johnson, gentleman, adventurer,
Braggart, minstrel, lover of a brawl,
Walked in the timber from Northfield to Hudson.
(Backward, forward, and sashay all!)
Old Dick Johnson, joker and wanderer,
Poet, vagabond, and beater of the track,
Sang a song of his bravery and prowess:
(Ladies go forward and gents go back!)

Chorus: *Ripsi, rantsi,*
   Humpsy, dumpsy;
   I, Dick Johnson,
   Killed Tecumseh!

Old Dick Johnson, fighter of the Indians,
Sang from Boston to the hills of Bath;
Sang the song of his muscle and his musket.
(Swing your partners and leave a path!)
The redskin sleeps where the wheat is growing,
But old Dick Johnson's ghost is free,
And it sings all night from Richfield to Twinsburg:
(All hands 'round with a one-two-three!)

Chorus: *Ripsi, rantsi,*
   Humpsy, dumpsy;
   I, Dick Johnson,
   Killed Tecumseh!

          Jake Falstaff

14

Greer County

How happy am I when I crawl into bed—
A rattlesnake hisses a tune at my head,
A gay little centipede, all without fear,
Crawls over my pillow and into my ear.

My clothes is all raggèd as my language is rough,
My bread is corndodgers, both solid and tough;
But yet I am happy, and live at my ease
On sorghum molasses, bacon, and cheese.

Good-by to Greer County where blizzards arise,
Where the sun never sinks and a flea never dies,
And the wind never ceases but always remains
Till it starves us to death on our government claims.

Farewell to Greer County, farewell to the West,
I'll travel back East to the girl I love best,
I'll travel back to Texas and marry me a wife,
And quit corn bread for the rest of my life.

Anonymous

Geronimo

Beside that tent and under guard
In majesty alone he stands,
As some chained eagle, broken-winged,
With eyes that gleam like smoldering brands,—
A savage face, streaked o'er with paint,
And coal-black hair in unkempt mane,
Thin, cruel lips, set rigidly,—
A red Apache Tamerlane.

As restless as the desert winds,
Yet here he stands like carven stone,
His raven locks by breezes moved
And backward o'er his shoulders blown;
Silent, yet watchful as he waits
Robed in his strange, barbaric guise,
While here and there go searchingly
The catlike wanderings of his eyes.

The eagle feather on his head
Is dull with many a bloody stain,
While darkly on his lowering brow
Forever rests the mark of Cain.
Have you but seen a tiger caged
And sullen through his barriers glare?
Mark well his human prototype,
The fierce Apache fettered there.

Ernest McGaffey

John Hardy

John Hardy was a brave and a desperate boy,
Said he carried two guns every day.
He shot him a man in the Shawnee camp,
And I seen John gettin' away, poor boy!
And I seen John Hardy gettin' away.

John Hardy had a little lovin' wife,
And children he had three,
But he cared no more for his wife and babes,
Than he cared for the rocks in the sea, poor boy!
Than he cared for the rocks in the sea.

16

John Hardy was a-standin' by the dark sea bar,
He was unconcerned in the game,
Up stepped a yaller girl with twenty dollars in her hand,
Said: "Deal John Hardy in the game, poor boy!"
Said: "Deal John Hardy in the game."

John Hardy stepped up with the money in his hand,
Sayin': "I have money for to play,
And the one who wins this yaller girl's dough,
I have powder to blow him away, poor boy!
I have powder to blow him away."

The cards was dealt and the money on the board.
Dave Campbell won that twenty-dollar bill.
John Hardy drew his pistol and took sure aim and fired,
And he caused Dave Campbell's brains to spill, poor boy!
And he caused Dave Campbell's brains to spill.

John Hardy had twelve mile to go
And six of them he ran.
He ran, he came to the river bank,
Then he fell on his bosom and he swam, poor boy!
Then he fell on his bosom and he swam.

John Hardy went to this big long town,
And he thought he was out of the way.
Up stepped a marshal and took him by the hand,
Says: "John Hardy, come and go with me, poor boy!"
Says: "John Hardy, come and go with me."

John Hardy's wife was dressed in blue.
She came for to go his bail.
No bail was allowed for murderin' a man,
So they put John Hardy back in jail, poor boy!
So they put John Hardy back in jail.

John Hardy stood in the middle of his cell,
And the tears run down his eyes,
Says: "I've been the death of many a man
And now I am ready for to die, poor boy!
And now I am ready for to die.

I've been to the East, I've been to the West,
I've traveled this wide world round.
I've been down to the river and I've been baptized,
So take me to the hangin' ground, poor boy!
So take me to the hangin' ground."

American ballad

The Bullwhacker

I'm a lonely bullwhacker
On the Red Cloud line.
I kin lick any son of a gun
Tries to yoke an ox of mine.
An' ef I kin catch him,
You bet I will or try,
I'll lick him with an oxbow,
Root, hog, or die.

It's out on the trail
With a dern heavy load,
With a contrary team
An' a muddy old road.
You may whip, you may holler,
You may cuss on the sly,
An' whack the cattle on, boys,
Root, hog, or die.

It's out on the trail,
These sights to be seen:
The ant'lope, the buffalo,
The prairie so green.
The ant'lope, the buffalo,
The rabbit jump so high,
So whack the cattle on, boys,
Root, hog, or die.

It's every day at twelve,
There's somethin' fer to do,
An' if it's nothin' else
There's a pony to shoe.
I'll throw down that pony
An' still make him lie.
Little pig, big pig,
Root, hog, or die.

Now p'raps you'd like to know
What we have to eat:
A little bit of bread
An' a little dirty meat,
A little black coffee
An' whisky on the sly,
So whack the cattle on, boys,
Root, hog, or die.

There's hard times on Bitter Creek,
That never kin be beat.
It was root, hog, or die
Under every wagon sheet.
We cleaned up the Injuns,
Drank all the alkali,
An' we whacked the cattle on, boys,
Root, hog, or die.

American ballad

The Insult

I've swum the Colorado where she runs close down to hell;
I've braced the faro layouts in Cheyenne;
I've fought for muddy water with a bunch of howlin'
    swine
An' swallowed hot tamales and cayenne.

I've rode a pitchin' bronco till the sky was underneath;
I've tackled every desert in the land;
I've sampled XX whisky till I couldn't hardly see
An' dallied with the quicksands of the Grande.

I've argued with the marshals of a half a dozen burgs;
I've been dragged free and fancy by a cow;
I've had three years' campaignin' with the fightin' bitin'
    Ninth,
An' I never lost my temper till right now.

I've had the yeller fever and been shot plumb full of holes;
I've grabbed an army mule plumb by the tail;
But I've never been so snortin', really highfalutin' mad
As when you up and hands me ginger ale.

American cowboy ballad

20

Lament for the Cowboy Life

Where the trails met, our herds met too,
And mingled on their lowing way to slaughter.
Spying ahead, the sky a parching blue,
We tortured valleys for their news of water.

And water found, we shared our food.
And settling by one fire watched nights together.
Waking each day to coffee freshly brewed
I never hungered for more gentle weather.

When outlaws ambushed us, we blazed them back,
We flushed them out, like partridges, from cover.
A double grave means someone's grief and lack,
But who they were the desert can discover.

Coming at last down to railhead
We sorted herds and haggled for fair prices.
The hands reported not one beast was dead,
Their massive flanks shipped off for butchers' slices.

And you had business there, and mine was on,
Three thousand miles across this continent.
And so we parted, partners, business done,
And whisky pledged our friendship permanent.

From Salem to Salinas grows this land,
And Massachusetts grass grows dollar-green.
And yet I wish I'd stayed a cattle hand
And never knew a country lies between.

Against my office window bumps the sun.
Now God herds us, as we those cattle then.
But every evening, on the homeward run,
I ride with cowboys, not with subway men.

Julian Mitchell

The Society upon the Stanislaus

I reside at Table Mountain, and my name is Truthful
    James;
I am not up to small deceit or any sinful games;
And I'll tell in simple language what I know about the row
That broke up our Society upon the Stanislow.

But first I would remark, that it is not a proper plan
For any scientific gent to whale his fellow man,
And, if a member don't agree with his peculiar whim,
To lay for that same member for to "put a head" on him.

Now nothing could be finer or more beautiful to see
Than the first six months' proceedings of that same Society,
Till Brown of Calaveras brought a lot of fossil bones
That he found within a tunnel near the tenement of Jones.

Then Brown he read a paper, and he reconstructed there,
From those same bones, an animal that was extremely rare;
And Jones then asked the Chair for a suspension of the
    rules,
Till he could prove that those same bones was one of his
    lost mules.

Then Brown he smiled a bitter smile, and said he was at
    fault,
It seemed he had been trespassing on Jones's family vault;
He was a most sarcastic man, this quiet Mr. Brown,
And on several occasions he had cleaned out the town.

Now I hold it is not decent for a scientific gent
To say another is an ass—at least, to all intent;
Nor should the individual who happens to be meant
Reply by heaving rocks at him, to any great extent.

Then Abner Dean of Angel's raised a point of order, when
A chunk of old red sandstone took him in the abdomen,
And he smiled a kind of sickly smile, and curled up on the
    floor,
And the subsequent proceedings interested him no more.

For, in less time than I write it, every member did engage
In a warfare with the remnants of a paleozoic age;
And the way they heaved those fossils in their anger was
    a sin,
Till the skull of an old mammoth caved the head of
    Thompson in.

And this is all I have to say of these improper games,
For I live at Table Mountain, and my name is Truthful
    James;
And I've told in simple language what I know about the
    row
That broke up our Society upon the Stanislow.

                                        Bret Harte

Proud Riders

We rode hard, and brought the cattle from brushy springs,
From heavy dying thickets, leaves wet as snow;
From high places, white-grassed, and dry in the wind;
Draws where the quaken-asps were yellow and white,
And the leaves spun and spun like money spinning.
We poured them out on the trail, and rode for town.

Men in the fields leaned forward in the wind,
Stood in the stubble and watched the cattle passing.
The wind bowed all, the stubble shook like a shirt.
We threw the reins by the yellow and black fields, and
    rode,
And came, riding together, into the town
Which is by the gray bridge, where the alders are.

The white-barked alder trees dropping big leaves,
Yellow and black, into the cold black water.
Children, little cold boys, watched after us—
The freezing wind flapped their clothes like windmill
    paddles.
Down the flat frosty road we crowded the herd:
High stepped the horses for us, proud riders in autumn.

H. L. Davis

Rodeo

Leathery, wry, and rough,
Jaw full of chaw, and slits
For eyes—this guy is tough.

He climbs the slatted fence,
Pulls himself atop and sits;
Tilts back his cowboy hat,
Stained with sweat below
The crown, and wipes a dirty
Sleeve across his brow;
Then pulls the hat down tight,
Caresses up its sides,
And spits into the dust
A benediction.

Gracelessly, his Brahma bull
Lunges into the chute
And swings a baleful
Eye around, irresolute.

Vision narrower still,
The man regards the beast.
There's weight enough to kill,
Bone and muscle fit at least
To jar a man apart.
The cowboy sniffs and hitches at
His pants. Himself all heart
And gristle, he watches as
The hands outside the chute
Prepare the sacrificial act.
Standing now, and nerving up,
He takes his final measure
Of the creature's awful back.

Then he moves. Swerving up
And into place, he pricks
The Brahma's bullish pride.

The gate swings free, and
Screams begin to sanctify
Their pitching, tortured ride.

Edward Lueders

Spanish Johnny

The old West, the old time,
  The old wind singing through
The red, red grass a thousand miles—
  And, Spanish Johnny, you!
He'd sit beside the water ditch
  When all his herd was in,
And never mind a child, but sing
  To his mandolin.

The big stars, the blue night,
  The moon-enchanted lane;
The olive man who never spoke,
  But sang the songs of Spain.
His speech with men was wicked talk—
  To hear it was a sin;
But those were golden things he said
  To his mandolin.

The gold songs, the gold stars,
  The world so golden then;
And the hand so tender to a child—
  Had killed so many men.
He died a hard death long ago
  Before the Road came in—

The night before he swung, he sang
  To his mandolin.

                              Willa Cather

Cowboy Song

I come from Salem County
  Where the silver melons grow,
Where the wheat is sweet as an angel's feet
  And the zithering zephyrs blow.
I walk the blue bone-orchard
  In the apple-blossom snow,
When the teasy bees take their honeyed ease
  And the marmalade moon hangs low.

My Maw sleeps prone on the prairie
  In a boulder eiderdown,
Where the pickled stars in their little jam jars
  Hang in a hoop to town.
I haven't seen Paw since a Sunday
  In eighteen seventy-three
When he packed his snap in a bitty mess trap
  And said he'd be home by tea.

Fled is my fancy sister
  All weeping like the willow,
And dead is the brother I loved like no other
  Who once did share my pillow.
I fly the florid water
  Where run the seven geese round,
O the townsfolk talk to see me walk
  Six inches off the ground.

Across the map of midnight
  I trawl the turning sky,
In my green glass the salt fleets pass
  The moon her fire-float by.
The girls go gay in the valley
  When the boys come down from the farm,
Don't run, my joy, from a poor cowboy,
  I won't do you no harm.

The bread of my twentieth birthday
  I buttered with the sun,
Though I sharpen my eyes with lovers' lies
  I'll never see twenty-one.
Light is my shirt with lilies,
  And lined with lead my hood,
On my face as I pass is a plate of brass,
  And my suit is made of wood.

Charles Causley

The Streets of Laredo

As I walked out in the streets of Laredo,
As I walked out in Laredo one day,
I spied a young cowboy all wrapped in white linen,
All wrapped in white linen as cold as the clay.

"I see by your outfit that you are a cowboy"—
These words he did say as I boldly stepped by,
"Come sit down beside me and hear my sad story;
I'm shot in the breast and I know I must die.

"It was once in the saddle I used to go dashing,
Once in the saddle I used to go gay;
First to the alehouse and then to the jailhouse,
Got shot in the breast and I'm dying today.

"Get six jolly cowboys to carry my coffin;
Get six pretty maidens to carry my pall;
Put bunches of roses all over my coffin,
Roses to deaden the clods as they fall.

"Oh, beat the drum slowly and play the fife lowly,
Play the dead march as you carry me along;
Take me to the green valley and lay the sod o'er me,
For I'm a young cowboy and I know I've done wrong.

"Go gather around you a crowd of young cowboys
And tell them the story of this, my sad fate;
Tell one and the other before they go further
To stop their wild roving before it's too late.

"Go fetch me a cup, a cup of cold water
To cool my parched lips," the cowboy then said.
Before I returned, the spirit had left him
And gone to its Maker—the cowboy was dead.

We beat the drum slowly and played the fife lowly,
And bitterly wept as we carried him along;
For we all loved our comrade, so brave, young, and
    handsome,
We all loved our comrade although he'd done wrong.

American ballad

Hell in Texas

The devil, we're told, in hell was chained,
And a thousand years he there remained,
And he never complained, nor did he groan,
But determined to start a hell of his own
Where he could torment the souls of men
Without being chained to a prison pen.

So he asked the Lord if He had on hand
Anything left when He made the land.
The Lord said, "Yes, I had plenty on hand,
But I left it down on the Rio Grande.
The fact is, old boy, the stuff is so poor,
I don't think you could use it in hell any more."

But the devil went down to look at the truck,
And said if it came as a gift, he was stuck;
For after examining it careful and well
He concluded the place was too dry for hell.
So in order to get it off His hands
God promised the devil to water the lands.

For he had some water, or rather some dregs,
A regular cathartic that smelt like bad eggs.
Hence the deal was closed and the deed was given,
And the Lord went back to His place in Heaven.
And the devil said, "I have all that is needed
To make a good hell," and thus he succeeded.

He began to put thorns on all the trees,
And he mixed the sand with millions of fleas,
He scattered tarantulas along all the roads,

Put thorns on the cacti and horns on the toads;
He lengthened the horns of the Texas steers
And put an addition on jack rabbits' ears.

He put little devils in the bronco steed
And poisoned the feet of the centipede.
The rattlesnake bites you, the scorpion stings,
The mosquito delights you by buzzing his wings.
The sand burrs prevail, so do the ants,
And those that sit down need half soles on their pants.

The devil then said that throughout the land
He'd manage to keep up the devil's own brand,
And all would be mavericks unless they bore
The marks of scratches and bites by the score.
The heat in the summer is a hundred and ten,
Too hot for the devil and too hot for men.

The wild boar roams through the black chaparral,
It's a hell of a place he has for a hell;
The red pepper grows by the bank of the brook,
The Mexicans use it in all that they cook.
Just dine with a Mexican and then you will shout,
"I've a hell on the inside as well as without."

Anonymous

'Dobe Bill

'Dobe Bill, he came a-riding
    From the canyon, in the glow
Of a quiet Sunday morning
    From the town of Angelo;
Ridin' easy on the pinto
    That he dearly loved to straddle,

With a six-gun and sombrero
    That was wider than his saddle.
And he's hummin' as he's ridin'
    Of a simple little song
That's a-rumblin' through the cactus
    As he's gallopin' along:

"Oh, I've rid from San Antony
    Through the mesquite and the sand,
I'm a r'arin', flarin' bucko,
    Not afraid to play my hand.
I'm a hootin', shootin' demon
    And I has my little fun
With my pinto called Apache
    And Adolphus—that's my gun."

Straight to Santa Fe he drifted,
    And he mills around the town,
Sorta gittin' of his bearin's
    While he pours his liquor down.
But he's watchin'—always watchin'—
    Every hombre in the place,
Like he's mebbe sorta lookin'
    For some certain hombre's face.

Then one night he saunters careless
    To the place of "Monte Sam,"
And he does a bit of playin'
    Like he doesn't give a damn.
All at once it's still and quiet
    Like a calm before a blow,
And the crowd is tense and nervous,
    And the playin's stopped and slow.

At the bar, a man is standin'
　　Sneerin' as his glances lay.
Like a challenge did he fling 'em,
　　Darin' 'em to make a play.
"Two-Gun" Blake, the Pecos killer,
　　Hated, feared wherever known,
Stood and drank his glass of mescal
　　With assurance all his own.

Then the eyes of Blake, the killer,
　　Caught the glance of 'Dobe Bill,
And they held each one the other
　　With the steel of looks that kill.
Then the tones of Blake came slowly,
　　With a sneer in every word:
"Well, you've found me!" But the other
　　Gave no sign he saw or heard.

Walkin' calmly toward the speaker,
　　He advanced with steady pace.
Then he grinned and quick as lightnin'
　　Slapped him squarely in the face.
"Shoot, you snake!" he whispered hoarsely.
　　"Shoot, you lily-livered cur!
Draw! You're always strong for killin';
　　Now I'm here to shoot for her!"

Some there was that claimed they saw it,
　　As the killer tried to draw—
But there's no one knows for certain
　　Just exactly what they saw.
I'll agree the shootin' started
　　Quick as Blake had made his start—

Then a brace of bullets hit him
   Fair and certain through the heart.

As he fell, his hand was graspin'
   Of the gun he'd got too late,
With the notches on it shown'
   Like the vagaries of Fate.
And the man who stood there lookin'
   At the killer as he lay,
Murmured: "Nell, I've kept my promise.
   I have made the scoundrel pay!"

'Dobe Bill, he went a-ridin'
   From the town of Santa Fe
On a quiet Sunday morning,
   Goin' happy on his way,
Ridin' happy on that pinto
   That he dearly loved to straddle,
With his six-gun and sombrero
   That was wider than his saddle.
And he's hummin' as he's goin'
   Of a simple little song
That's a-boomin' through the cactus
   As he's gallopin' along:

"Oh, I'm goin' down the valley,
   Through the mesquite and the sand.
I'm a r'arin', flarin' bucko,
   Not afraid to play my hand.
I'm a hootin', shootin' demon
   And I has my little fun
With my bronco called Apache
   And Adolphus—that's my gun."

American cowboy song

34

Tying a Knot in the Devil's Tail

Way up high in the Syree Peaks
Where the yellow pines grow tall,
Old Sandy Bob and Buster Jiggs
Had a round-up camp last fall.

They took their horses and their runnin' irons
And maybe a dog or two;
And they 'lowed they'd brand all the long-eared calves
That came within their view.

Many a long-eared dogie
That didn't hush up by day
Had his long ears whittled and his old hide scorched
In a most artistic way.

One fine day, says Buster Jiggs
As he throwed his cigo down,
"I'm tired o' cow-piography
And I 'lows I'm goin' to town."

So they saddles up and they hits a lope
Fer it wa'n't no sight of a ride,
And them was the days that a good cowpunch'
Could ile up his inside.

They started her in at the Kentucky Bar
At the head of Whisky Row
And ends her up at the Depot House,
Some forty drinks below.

They sets her up and they turns around
And goes her the other way;
An' to tell the Godforsaken truth
Them boys got tight that day.

When they were on their way to camp
A-packin' a pretty good load,
Who should they meet but the Devil hisself
Come a-prancin' down the road.

Says he, "Ye ornery cowboy skunks,
Ye'd better hunt for your holes,
'Cause I've come up from hell's rimrock
To gather in your souls."

Says Buster Jiggs: "The Devil be damned!
We boys are feelin' kinda tight,
But you don't gather any cowboy souls
Unless you want a fight."

So he punches a hole in his old cigo
And he throws her straight and true
An' he loops it over the Devil's horns
An' he takes his dallies true.

Old Sandy Bob was a riata man
With his gut line coiled up neat,
But he shakes her out, an' builds a loop
An' he ropes the Devil's hind feet.

They stretches him out and they tails him down,
An' while their irons were gettin' hot
They cropped and swallow-forked his ears
An' branded him up a lot.

They prunes him up with a dehorning saw
An' they knotted his tail for a joke;
An' then they rode off an' left him there
Tied up to a lilac-jack oak.

Now when you're way up high in the Syree Peaks
An' you hear one hell of a wail,
It's only the Devil a-bellerin' round
About those knots in his tail.

Anonymous

SEA DOGS AND BUCCANEERS

Storm at Sea

Blow! blow! The winds are so hoarse they cannot blow!
Cold! cold! Our tears freeze to hail, our spittle to snow!
The waves are all up, they swell as they run!
     Let them rise and rise,
     As high as the skies,
And higher to wash the face of the sun.

Port! port! The pilot is blind. Port at the helm!
Yare! yare! For one foot of shore take a whole realm!
A-lee, or we sink! Does no man know how to wind her?
     Less noise and more room!
     We sail in a drum!
Our sails are but rags, which lightning turns to tinder.

Aloof! aloof! Hey how those carracks and ships
Fall foul and are tumbled and driven like chips!
Our boatswain, alas! a silly weak gristle,
     For fear to catch cold,
     Lies down in the hold,
We all hear his sighs but few hear his whistle.

Sir William Davenant

1805

At Viscount Nelson's lavish funeral,
  While the mob milled and yelled about St. Paul's,
A General chatted with an Admiral:

"One of your Colleagues, Sir, remarked today
  That Nelson's *exit*, though to be lamented,
Falls not inopportunely, in its way."

"He was a thorn in our flesh," came the reply—
  "The most bird-witted, unaccountable,
Odd little runt that ever I did spy..

"One arm, one peeper, vain as Pretty Poll,
  A meddler, too, in foreign politics
And gave his heart in pawn to a plain moll.

"He would dare lecture us Sea Lords, and then
  Would treat his ratings as though men of honor
And play at leapfrog with his midshipmen!

"We tried to box him down, but up he popped,
  And when he'd banged Napoleon at the Nile
Became too much the hero to be dropped.

"You've heard that Copenhagen 'blind eye' story?
  We'd tied him to Nurse Parker's apron-strings—
By God, he snipped them through and snatched the glory!"

"Yet," cried the General, "six-and-twenty sail
  Captured or sunk by him off Tráfalgár—
That writes a handsome *finis* to the tale."

42

"Handsome enough. The seas are England's now.
That fellow's foibles need no longer plague us.
He died most creditably, I'll allow."

"And, Sir, the secret of his victories?"
"By his unServicelike, familiar ways, Sir,
He made the whole Fleet love him, damn his eyes!"

Robert Graves

The Bashful Man

As I were standin' on the sand a-watchin' of the brine,
A hefty pebble hit me in the middle of my spine;
And thar behind a dory p'intin' nor-nor'west by south
I found a blushin' feller with his finger in his mouth.

Sez I, "Be you a-hidin' here from accident er choice?"
An' I shook him by the riggin' jest to loosen up his voice.
I further sez, "Be you the cove thet hove a rock at me?"
He hemmed an' hawed awhile, an' chawed his nail, an' sez,
    sez he:

"I'm a werry, werry bashful man, as one might truly say;
I git embarrassed orful when a stranger looks my way.
So when I long fer doin's with my feller human kind,
I'm much too shy to meet their eye, but soak 'em from
    behind.

"It's werry hard on me, indeed, to hev sich shrinkin'
    ways,—
I've hed a bent fer argument through all my livelong days.

But when I think thet folks is wrong in anything they
    claim,
I tell 'em so on postal cards an' never sign my name.

"I allers act on impulse, an' I love a lynchin' job;
But I'm so shy I allers try to mingle in the mob;
The thought of offerin' to treat jest scares me to the bone,
So, though I'm friendly as kin be, I allers drink alone.

"So now," sez he, "I'm sure you'll see, from knowin' of my
    mind,
'Twas in a shyly playful way I lammed you from behind."
"I bear no grudge at all," sez I, "your tale is werry rum;
Your skin is much too thin," I sez, "it should be toughened
    some."

I tanned him with a dory thwart, I rubbed him in the sand,
I propped him up agin an oar, it tired him so to stand.
I chucked him neatly in the wet, I dried him in the sun;
Sez I, "I'm sure 'twill be a cure, you'll thank me when I'm
    done."

We meet no more along the shore upon my daily stroll;
I like ter think I've ben a help to one pore mortal soul.
I sort of guess I cured him—er else I recken he
Is so werry, werry bashful thet he keeps away from me.

Burges Johnson

The Revenge

A Ballad of the Fleet

I

At Flores in the Azores Sir Richard Grenville lay,
And a pinnace, like a fluttered bird, came flying from far
away:
"Spanish ships of war at sea! We have sighted fifty-three!"
Then sware Lord Thomas Howard: " 'Fore God I am no
coward;
But I cannot meet them here, for my ships are out of gear,
And the half my men are sick. I must fly, but follow quick.
We are six ships of the line; can we fight with fifty-three?"

II

Then spake Sir Richard Grenville: "I know you are no
coward;
You fly them for a moment to fight with them again.
But I've ninety men and more that are lying sick ashore.
I should count myself the coward if I left them, my Lord
Howard,
To these Inquisition dogs and the devildoms of Spain."

III

So Lord Howard passed away with five ships of war that
day,
Till he melted like a cloud in the silent summer heaven;
But Sir Richard bore in hand all his sick men from the land
Very carefully and slow,
Men of Bideford in Devon,
And we laid them on the ballast down below;

For we brought them all aboard,
And they blessed him in their pain, that they were not left
to Spain,
To the thumbscrew and the stake, for the glory of the Lord.

IV

He had only a hundred seamen to work the ship and to
fight,
And he sailed away from Flores till the Spaniard came in
sight,
With his huge sea-castles heaving upon the weather bow.
"Shall we fight or shall we fly?
Good Sir Richard, tell us now,
For to fight is but to die!
There'll be little of us left by the time this sun be set."
And Sir Richard said again: "We be all good English men.
Let us bang these dogs of Seville, the children of the devil,
For I never turned my back upon Don or devil yet."

V

Sir Richard spoke and he laughed, and we roared a hurrah,
and so
The little *Revenge* ran on sheer into the heart of the foe,
With her hundred fighters on deck, and her ninety sick
below;
For half of their fleet to the right and half to the left were
seen,
And the little *Revenge* ran on through the long sea-lane
between.

VI

Thousands of their soldiers looked down from their decks
and laughed,
Thousands of their seamen made mock at the mad little
craft

46

Running on and on, till delayed
By their mountain-like *San Philip* that, of fifteen hundred
    tons,
And up-shadowing high above us with her yawning tiers
    of guns,
Took the breath from our sails, and we stayed.

      VII
And while now the great *San Philip* hung above us like a
    cloud
Whence the thunderbolt will fall
Long and loud,
Four galleons drew away
From the Spanish fleet that day,
And two upon the larboard and two upon the starboard lay,
And the battle thunder broke from them all.

      VIII
But anon the great *San Philip*, she bethought herself and
    went,
Having that within her womb that had left her ill content;
And the rest they came aboard us, and they fought us hand
    to hand,
For a dozen times they came with their pikes and
    musketeers
And a dozen times we shook 'em off as a dog that shakes
    his ears
When he leaps from the water to the land.

      IX
And the sun went down, and the stars came out far over
    the summer sea,
But never a moment ceased the fight of the one and the
    fifty-three.

Ship after ship, the whole night long, their high-built
    galleons came,
Ship after ship, the whole night long, with her battle
    thunder and flame;
Ship after ship, the whole night long, drew back with her
    dead and her shame.
For some were sunk and many were shattered, and so could
    fight us no more—
God of battles, was ever a battle like this in the world
    before?

        x
For he said, "Fight on! fight on!"
Though his vessel was all but a wreck;
And it chanced that, when half of the short summer night
    was gone,
With a grisly wound to be dressed he had left the deck,
But a bullet struck him that was dressing it suddenly dead,
And himself he was wounded again in the side and the
    head,
And he said, "Fight on! fight on!"

        xi
And the night went down, and the sun smiled out far over
    the summer sea,
And the Spanish fleet with broken sides lay round us all in
    a ring;
But they dared not touch us again, for they feared that we
    still could sting,
So they watched what the end would be.
And we had not fought them in vain,
But in perilous plight were we,
Seeing forty of our poor hundred were slain,
And half of the rest of us maimed for life

48

In the crash of the cannonades and the desperate strife;
And the sick men down in the hold were most of them
   stark and cold,
And the pikes were all broken or bent, and the powder was
   all of it spent;
And the masts and the rigging were lying over the side;
But Sir Richard cried in his English pride,
"We have fought such a fight for a day and a night
As may never be fought again!
We have won great glory, my men!
And a day less or more
At sea or ashore,
We die—does it matter when?
Sink me the ship, Master Gunner—sink her, split her in
   twain!
Fall into the hands of God, not into the hands of Spain!"

XII

And the gunner said, "Aye, aye," but the seamen made
   reply:
"We have children, we have wives,
And the Lord hath spared our lives.
We will make the Spaniard promise, if we yield, to let us
   go;
We shall live to fight again and to strike another blow."
And the lion there lay dying, and they yielded to the foe.

XIII

And the stately Spanish men to their flagship bore him then,
Where they laid him by the mast, old Sir Richard caught at
   last,
And they praised him to his face with their courtly foreign
   grace;
But he rose upon their decks, and he cried:

"I have fought for Queen and Faith like a valiant man and
    true;
I have only done my duty as a man is bound to do:
With a joyful spirit I Sir Richard Grenville die!"
And he fell upon their decks, and he died.

                XIV
And they stared at the dead that had been so valiant and
    true,
And had holden the power and glory of Spain so cheap
That he dared her with one little ship and his English few;
Was he devil or man? He was devil for aught they knew,
But they sank his body with honor down into the deep,
And they manned the *Revenge* with a swarthier alien crew,
And away she sailed with her loss and longed for her own;
When a wind from the lands they had ruined awoke from
    sleep,
And the water began to heave and the weather to moan,
And or ever that evening ended a great gale blew,
And a wave like the wave that is raised by an earthquake
    grew,
Till it smote on their hulls and their sails and their masts
    and their flags,
And the whole sea plunged and fell on the shot-shattered
    navy of Spain,
And the little *Revenge* herself went down by the island
    crags
To be lost evermore in the main.

                                Alfred, Lord Tennyson

        50

Admirals All

Effingham, Grenville, Raleigh, Drake,
    Here's to the bold and free!
Benbow, Collingwood, Byron, Blake,
    Hail to the Kings of the Sea!
Admirals all, for England's sake,
    Honor be yours and fame!
And honor, as long as waves shall break,
    To Nelson's peerless name!

> *Admirals all, for England's sake,*
>   *Honor be yours and fame!*
> *And honor, as long as waves shall break,*
>   *To Nelson's peerless name!*

Essex was fretting in Cadiz Bay
    With the galleons fair in sight;
Howard at last must give him his way,
    And the word was passed to fight.
Never was schoolboy gayer than he,
    Since holidays first began:
He tossed his bonnet to wind and sea,
    And under the guns he ran.

Drake nor devil nor Spaniard feared,
    Their cities he put to the sack!
He signed His Catholic Majesty's beard,
    And harried his ships to wrack.
He was playing at Plymouth a rubber of bowls
    When the great Armada came!
But he said, "They must wait their turn, good souls,"
    And he stooped, and finished the game.

Fifteen sail were the Dutchmen bold,
    Duncan he had but two:
But he anchored them fast where the Texel shoaled,
    And his colors aloft he flew.
"I've taken the depth to a fathom," he cried,
    "And I'll sink with a right good will,
For I know when we're all of us under the tide,
    My flag will be fluttering still."

Splinters were flying above, below,
    When Nelson sailed the Sound:
"Mark you, I wouldn't be elsewhere now,"
    Said he, "for a thousand pound!"
The Admiral's signal bade him fly,
    But he wickedly wagged his head,
He clapped the glass to his sightless eye,
    And "I'm damned if I see it!" he said.

Admirals all, they said their say
    (The echoes are ringing still),
Admirals all, they went their way
    To the haven under the hill.
But they left us a kingdom none can take,
    The realm of the circling sea,
To be ruled by the rightful sons of Blake
    And the Rodneys yet to be.

> *Admirals all, for England's sake,*
>   *Honor be yours and fame!*
> *And honor, as long as waves shall break,*
>   *To Nelson's peerless name!*

                                        Henry Newbolt

The Deckhands

There's some is bums from city slums
That ain't so strong on knowledge;
There's some that hails from county jails
An' some that hails from college;
There's some is mild an' some is wild
An' some is smart an' chipper—
The kind that climbs an' gets, sometimes,
To be a mate or skipper.

A lousy lot
You'll say, an' not
What you'd consider what is what;
Well, yes, we lack
A high shellac
But we're not meant for bric-a-brac.

Believe me, pard, we're rough and hard
An' scarcely things of beauty;
We're never made for dress parade
But just for heavy duty;
To strain our spines at handlin' lines—
To do our stint of swabbin'—
When combers roll to pass the coal
To keep the screws a-throbbin'.

It's true we ain't
Exactly "quaint"
Like "hale old salts" the painters paint,
But we can do
The work for you—
An' that's the business of a crew.

We're single guys without no ties
Of any kind to bind us,
Tho' I can't state the aggregate
Of girls we've left behind us.
In port we drink an' get in "clink"
In spite of ev'ry warnin'—
Our money spent, we're all content
To ship again next mornin'.

The mate may rare
An' swear an' tear—
Us deckhands doesn't greatly care,
For kicks an' blame
Is in the game—
They've got to have us just the same.

November blows an' wintry snows
Don't find us any glummer,
We still can shirk our daily work
As well as in the summer.
For, so we gets our cigarettes
An' wages, when it's over
We'll take a trip in any ship
An' think ourselves in clover.

We wouldn't please
At balls or teas,
Where high-toned folks is what you sees;
But don't you doubt
This fact, old scout,
We're guys they can't get on without.

Anonymous

54

Harp Song of the Dane Women

What is a woman that you forsake her,
And the hearth-fire and the home-acre,
To go with the old gray Widow-maker?

She has no house to lay a guest in—
But one chill bed for all to rest in,
That the pale suns and the stray bergs nest in.

She has no strong white arms to fold you,
But the ten-times-fingering weed to hold you—
Out on the rocks where the tide has rolled you.

Yet, when the signs of summer thicken,
And the ice breaks, and the birch buds quicken,
Yearly you turn from our side, and sicken—

Sicken again for the shouts and the slaughters.
You steal away to the lapping waters,
And look at your ship in her winter quarters.

You forget our mirth, and talk at the tables,
The kine in the shed and the horse in the stables—
To pitch her sides and go over her cables.

Then you drive out where the storm clouds swallow,
And the sound of your oar blades, falling hollow,
Is all we have left through the months to follow.

Ah, what is Woman that you forsake her,
And the hearth-fire and the home-acre,
To go with the old gray Widow-maker?

Rudyard Kipling

The Sack of Old Panama

They sat in a tavern in wicked Port Royal,
Grim Morgan and Brodley and one or two others,
A flagon of rum on the table between them
And villainy binding them closer than brothers.

And Morgan dropped hint of Old Panama's riches;
Said little, but said it with evil suggestion,
Till Brodley swayed up, with his glass in his fingers,
And swore that a Don was an aid to digestion!

But Morgan said, idly, " 'Twould be a long journey—"
Cried Brodley: "What odds, when the end of it's yellow?
I mind me the pockets of dead men I lightened
That year of our Lord when we sacked Porto Bello!"

Then Morgan stood straight, with his face of dark smiling:
"I'll rake them once more—then I'll stop all such capers;
Come home and be Governor! Aye, but I will, though,
And hang every master that can't show his papers.

"I'll have me a house that will front the blue water,
And devil a pirate shall sit at my table;
But now, and once more, I've a will to go courting,
To dance with a Don while I'm hearty and able."

He laughed and drew breath; and they tipped up the
    flagon,
And fashioned his words in a stormy sea ditty.
Then swiftly fell silent, with dream-darkened faces,
And thought of their hands at the throat of a city. . . .

* * *

56

The sea was as blue as the breast of the morning
When Morgan went down to his last buccaneering;
His sails were like low-fallen clouds in the distance,
Blown onward, and fading, and slow disappearing.

And so he put out—and was part of the distance,
A blur of slow wings on the blue ring of heaven,
With two thousand devils adream below hatches,
And steel, and dry powder, and ships thirty-seven.

And all down the decks there was talk of the venture—
How Morgan had wind of unthinkable treasure;
How Panama's streets were the sweetness of silver,
Where men in gold gutters threw pearls for their pleasure!

And Brodley went forward and took San Lorenzo,
With patience and passion, as men take a woman,
And Morgan came up, with his face of dark smiling,
And saw the sword's kiss on the heart of the foeman.

*   *   *

The dawn saw them marching—twelve hundred brown
   devils,
With steel and dry powder and gay crimson sashes;
And so they put on . . . and were dead in the jungle
Of great shaking fevers and little barbs' gashes.

*   *   *

The tenth day was sleeping in tents of red splendor
When Morgan crept up to the walls of the city—
Behind him his madmen came shouting and sobbing,
And mouthing the words of an old pirate ditty.

Their souls were in tatters! And still they came singing,
Till all the hushed foreland was waked from its dreaming,
And high in their towers the sweet bells of vesper
Were drowned and made dim by the mad, measured
    screaming.

A gun roared, and deep in the heart of the city
Wild pulses began. . . . A young mother ran crying,
"The English are on us!" Swords silvered the twilight,
And priests turned their books to the prayers for the dying.

Then out from his gates came the desperate Spaniard;
The swords were like flame, and the towers were ringing!
But Morgan's men waited; lay down with choked muzzles,
And dealt out their death to the pulse of their singing.

Their volleys belched forth like a chorus of thunder,
A great whining Song that went on without pity,
Till night drew her veil . . . then they rose from their
    bellies,
And spat at the dead—and went into the city.

* * *

The Governor sat in his window at evening,
His window that looked on the star-furrowed water;
A ship had come into the clasp of the harbor,
Clear-lined from the darkness the bright moon had
    wrought her.

* * *

He clapped his fat hands; and a black lad stood bowing.
"Bring candles—and rum," said the Governor, grinning.
And then he sat down with his boots on the table,
And dozed until Morgan should come from his sinning. . . .

He came, with an oath, in his great greasy sea boots,
A sash at his waist, and a pistol stuck in it,
His beard to his throat, and his little eyes leering—
"Your voice," said Sir Thomas, "is sweet as a linnet!"

"My pockets are sweeter," said Morgan; and, winking,
He drew from his sash a creased bag of black leather,
Unloosed it and spilled on the bare wooden table
Red jewels that kindled like swords struck together!

*   *   *

The jewels lay warm in the dusk of the candles,
Like soulless red eyes that no tears might set blinking . . .
And Thomas Sir Modyford crooked his hot fingers,
And chose the King's profit, whilst Morgan sat drinking.

"Sweet baubles! Sweet pretties! They've blinded my
    candles.
They're flame, Pirate, flame! See my hand, how they've
    burned it."
He laughed, and drew forth from his pocket a parchment—
"It's yours, by our bargain; and damme, you've earned it."

They spread out the parchment between them. Said
    Morgan:
"God's name! I'm respectable!" "Aye," said Sir Thomas,
"Ye're Leftenant-Governor, lately appointed
By will of the Crown—in accord with our promise!"

*   *   *

Day broke . . . and the throat of the harbor was clouded
With sail. 'Twas the fleet of the pirates returning—
But down their grim ports no black muzzles peered
    frowning,
Nor naked steel leaped for the dawn to set burning.

59

They came as calm merchantmen, shriven with morning
(For in the King's harbors the law is hardfisted!)
And so they stole in, like whipped hounds to a kennel,
Their loosed anchors lolling like tongues when they listed.

The candles were dead in the Governor's chamber;
And in at the window the young light came creeping—
Asprawl at the table sat Morgan the Pirate,
And under his boot heels Sir Thomas lay sleeping.

The anchors splashed down in the ruffled blue water,
The great wings were furled with a rattle of gearing;
But Morgan sat clutching a folded gray parchment,
A glass at his lips, and his little eyes leering.

Dana Burnet

The Last Buccaneer

Oh England is a pleasant place for them that's rich and
    high,
But England is a cruel place for such poor folks as I;
And such a port for mariners I ne'er shall see again
As the pleasant Isle of Avès, beside the Spanish main.

There were forty craft in Avès that were both swift and
    stout,
All furnished well with small arms and cannons round
    about;
And a thousand men in Avès made laws so fair and free
To choose their valiant captains and obey them loyally.

Thence we sailed against the Spaniard with his hoards of
  plate and gold,
Which he wrung with cruel tortures from Indian folk of
  old;
Likewise the merchant captains, with hearts as hard as
  stone,
Who flog men and keelhaul them, and starve them to the
  bone.

Oh the palms grew high in Avès, and fruits that shone like
  gold,
And the colibris and parrots they were gorgeous to behold;
And the native maids to Avès from bondage fast did flee,
To welcome gallant sailors, a-sweeping in from sea.

Oh sweet it was in Avès to hear the landward breeze,
A-swing with good tobacco in a net between the trees,
With a native lass to fan you, while you listened to the roar
Of the breakers on the reef outside, that never touched the
  shore.

But Scripture saith, an ending to all fine things must be;
So the King's ships sailed on Avès, and quite put down
  were we.
All day we fought like bulldogs, but they burst the booms
  at night;
And I fled in a piragua, sore wounded, from the fight.

Nine days I floated starving, and a native lass beside,
Till for all I tried to cheer her, the poor young thing she
  died;
But as I lay a-gasping, a Bristol sail came by,
And brought me home to England here, to beg until I die.

And now I'm old and going—I'm sure I can't tell where;
One comfort is, this world's so hard, I can't be worse off
    there:
If I might but be a sea dove, I'd fly across the main,
To the pleasant Isle of Avès, to look at it once again.

Charles Kingsley

Admiral Death

Boys, are ye calling a toast tonight?
    (Hear what the sea wind saith)
Fill for a bumper strong and bright,
    And here's to Admiral Death!
He's sailed in a hundred builds o' boat,
He's fought in a thousand kinds o' coat,
He's the senior flag of all that float,
    And his name's Admiral Death!

Which of you looks for a service free?
    (Hear what the sea wind saith)
The rules of the service are but three
    When ye sail with Admiral Death.
Steady your hand in the time o' squalls,
Stand to the last by him that falls,
And answer clear to the voice that calls,
    "Aye, aye, Admiral Death!"

How will ye know him among the rest?
    (Hear what the sea wind saith)
By the glint o' the stars that cover his breast
    Ye may find Admiral Death.
By the forehead grim with an ancient scar,
By the voice that rolls like thunder far,

By the tenderest eyes of all that are,
   Ye may know Admiral Death.

Where are the lads that sailed before?
   (Hear what the sea wind saith)
Their bones are white by many a shore,
   They sleep with Admiral Death.
Oh! but they loved him, young and old,
For he left the laggard, and took the bold,
And the fight was fought, and the story's told,
   And they sleep with Admiral Death.

Henry Newbolt

Seumas Beg

A man was sitting underneath a tree
Outside the village; and he asked me what
Name was upon this place; and said that he
Was never here before—He told a lot

Of stories to me too. His nose was flat!
I asked him how it happened, and he said
—The first mate of the Holy Ghost did that
With a marling-spike one day; but he was dead,

And jolly good job too; and he'd have gone
A long way to have killed him—Oh, he had
A gold ring in one ear; the other one
—"Was bit off by a crocodile, bedad!"

That's what he said. He taught me how to chew!
He was a real nice man! He liked me too!

James Stephens

Tarpauling Jacket

I am a young jolly brisk sailor,
   Delights in all manner of sport,
When I'm in liquor I'm mellow,
   The girls I then merrily court.
But love is surrounded with trouble,
   And puts such strange thoughts in my head,
Is it not a terrible story,
   That love it should strike me stone dead?

Here's a health to my friends and acquaintance,
   When death for me it doth come,
And let them behave in their station
   And send me a cask of good rum,
Let it be good royal stingo,
   With three barrels of beer,
To make my friends the more welcome,
   When they meet me at derry down fair.

Let there be six sailors to carry me,
   And let them be damnable drunk,
And as they are going to bury me,
   Let them fall down with my trunk.
Let there be no sighing or sobbing,
   But one single favor I crave,
Take me up in a tarpauling jacket,
   And fiddle and dance to my grave.

Anonymous

The Crocodile

Now listen you landsmen unto me, to tell you the truth
  I'm bound,
What happened to me by going to sea, and the wonders
  that I found;
Shipwrecked I was once off Perouse and cast upon the
  shore,
So then I did resolve to roam, the country to explore.

'Twas far I had not scouted out, when close alongside the
  ocean,
I saw something move which at first I thought was all the
  world in motion;
But steering up close alongside, I found 'twas a crocodile,
And from his nose to the tip of his tail he measured five
  hundred mile.

While up aloft the wind was high, it blew a gale from the
  south,
I lost my hold and away did fly right into the crocodile's
  mouth,
He quickly closed his jaws on me and thought he'd got a
  victim,
But I ran down his throat, d'ye see, and that's the way I
  tricked him.

I traveled on for a month or two, till I got into his maw,
Where I found of rum kegs not a few, and a thousand fat
  bullocks in store.
Of life I banished all my care, for of grub I was not stinted,
And in this crocodile I lived ten years, and very well
  contented.

This crocodile being very old, one day, alas, he died;
He was ten long years a-getting cold, he was so long and
  wide,
His skin was eight miles thick, I'm sure, or very near about,
For I was full ten years or more a-cutting my way out.

And now I've once more got on earth, I've vowed no more
  to roam;
In a ship that passed I got a berth, and now I'm safe at
  home.
And if my story you should doubt, should you ever travel
  the Nile,
It's ten to one you'll find the shell of the wonderful crocodile.

Anonymous

Admiral Benbow

Come, all ye seamen bold
  And draw near, and draw near,
Come, listen to my song
  And have no fear:
'Tis of an Admiral's fame,
And John Benbow was his name—
How unto his end he came
  You shall hear, you shall hear.

John Benbow he set sail
  For to fight, for to fight,
Until Du Casse's ships
  They hove in sight.

66

He after them made sail
With a fine and pleasant gale,
But his captains they turned tail,
    In affright, in affright.

Said Kirby unto Wade:
    "Let us run! Let us run!"
To Kirby, Wade replied:
    "Aye, let's have done,
For I value no disgrace
Nor the losing of my place
But I swear I will not face
    Shot of gun, shot of gun!"

So brave Benbow sailed alone
    On that day, on that day.
Alone against the French,
    Where they lay;
He fought them with a frown,
Till the blood came trickling down—
And he earned a great renown
    On that day, on that day.

Brave Benbow lost his leg
    By chain shot, by chain shot;
Yet all the pain he bore
    He valued not;
Brave Benbow lost his leg
But his company he did beg:
"Fight on lads, don't reneg!
    'Tis our lot, 'tis our lot!"

A surgeon dressed his wound;
    Cried Benbow, cried Benbow:

"Nay, to my cabin, faith,
    I will not go!
Let a cradle[1] now in haste
On the quarter-deck be placed!"
And with a fury still he faced
    England's foe, England's foe.

Anonymous

---

[1] *cradle:* a support for his shattered leg

KNIGHTS AND DEEDS

Opportunity

This I beheld, or dreamed it in a dream:—
There spread a cloud of dust along the plain;
And underneath the cloud, or in it, raged
A furious battle, and men yelled, and swords
Shocked upon swords and shields. A prince's banner
Wavered, then staggered backward, hemmed by foes.
A craven hung along the battle's edge,
And thought: "Had I a sword of keener steel—
That blue blade that the king's son bears—but this
Blunt thing—!" He snapped and flung it from his hand,
And lowering crept away and left the field.
Then came the king's son, wounded, sore bestead,
And weaponless, and saw the broken sword,
Hilt-buried in the dry and trodden sand,
And ran and snatched it, and with battle shout
Lifted afresh he hewed his enemy down,
And saved a great cause that heroic day.

Edward Rowland Sill

A Flight Shot

We were twin brothers, tall and hale,
Glad wanderers over hill and dale.

We stood within the twilight shade
Of pines that rimmed a Southern glade.

He said: "Let's settle, if we can,
Which of us is the stronger man.

We'll try a flight shot, high and good,
Across the green glade toward the wood."

And so we bent in sheer delight
Our old yew bows with all our might.

Our long keen shafts, drawn to the head,
Were poised a moment ere they sped.

As we leaned back a breath of air
Mingled the brown locks of our hair.

We loosed. As one our bow cords rang,
As one away our arrows sprang.

Away they sprang; the wind of June
Thrilled to their softly whistled tune.

We watched their flight, and saw them strike
Deep in the ground slantwise alike,

So far away that they might pass
For two thin straws of broom-sedge grass!

Then arm in arm we doubting went
To find whose shaft was farthest sent,

Each fearing in his loving heart
That brother's shaft had fallen short.

But who could tell by such a plan
Which of us was the stronger man?

There at the margin of the wood,
Side by side our arrows stood,

Their red cock-feathers wing and wing,
Their amber nocks still quivering,

Their points deep-planted where they fell
An inch apart and parallel!

We clasped each other's hands; said he,
"Twin champions of the world are we!"

Maurice Thompson

Kate

I know her by her angry air,
Her bright black eyes, her bright black hair,
   Her rapid laughters wild and shrill,
As laughters of the woodpecker
   From the bosom of a hill.

'Tis Kate—she sayeth what she will:
For Kate hath an unbridled tongue,
   Clear as the twanging of a harp.
   Her heart is like a throbbing star.
Kate hath a spirit ever strung
   Like a new bow, and bright and sharp
   As edges of the scymetar.
Whence shall she take a fitting mate?
   For Kate no common love will feel;
My woman-soldier, gallant Kate,
   As pure and true as blades of steel.

Kate saith, "The world is void of might."
   Kate saith, "The men are gilded flies."
   Kate snaps her fingers at my vows;
Kate will not hear of lovers' sighs.
I would I were an armèd knight,
   Far-famed for well-won enterprise,
     And wearing on my swarthy brows
   The garland of new-wreathed emprise:
     For in a moment I would pierce
The blackest files of clanging fight,
And strongly strike to left and right,
   In dreaming of my lady's eyes.
     Oh! Kate loves well the bold and fierce;
   But none are bold enough for Kate,
   She cannot find a fitting mate.

              Alfred, Lord Tennyson

The Troubadour

A troubadour he played
  Without a castle wall;
Within, a hapless maid
  Responded to his call.

"Oh, willow, woe is me!
  Alack and welladay!
If I were only free
  I'd hie me far away!"

Unknown her face and name,
  But this he knew right well,
The maiden's wailing came
  From out a dungeon cell.

A hapless woman lay
  Within that prison grim—
That fact, I've heard him say,
  Was quite enough for him.

"I will not sit or lie,
  Or eat or drink, I vow,
Till thou art free as I,
  Or I as pent as thou!"

Her tears then ceased to flow,
  Her wails no longer rang,
And tuneful in her woe
  The prisoned maiden sang:

"Oh, stranger, as you play
    I recognize your touch;
And all that I can say,
    Is thank you very much!"

He seized his clarion straight,
    And blew thereat, until
A warder oped the gate,
    "Oh, what might be your will?"

"I've come, sir knave, to see
    The master of these halls:
A maid unwillingly
    Lies prisoned in their walls."

With barely stifled sigh
    That porter dropped his head,
With teardrops in his eye,
    "A many, sir," he said.

He stayed to hear no more,
    But pushed that porter by,
And shortly stood before
    SIR HUGH DE PECKHAM RYE.

SIR HUGH he darkly frowned,
    "What would you, sir, with me?"
The troubadour he downed
    Upon his bended knee.

"I've come, DE PECKHAM RYE,
    To do a Christian task,
You ask me what would I?
    It is not much I ask.

"Release these maidens, sir,
    Whom you dominion o'er—
Particularly her
    Upon the second floor!

"And if you don't, my lord"—
    He here stood bolt upright,
And tapped a tailor's sword—
    "Come out at once and fight!"

SIR HUGH he called—and ran
    The warden from the gate,
"Go, show this gentleman
    The maid in forty-eight."

By many a cell they passed
    And stopped at length before
A portal bolted fast:
    The man unlocked the door.

He called inside the gate
    With coarse and brutal shout,
"Come, step it, forty-eight!"
    And forty-eight stepped out.

"They gets it pretty hot,
    The maidens wot we cotch—
Two years this lady's got
    For collaring a wotch."

"Oh, ah!—indeed—I see,"
    The troubadour exclaimed—
"If I may make so free,
    How is this castle named?"

The warden's eyelids fill,
    And sighing, he replied,
"Of gloomy Pentonville
    This is the Female Side!"

The minstrel did not wait
    The warden stout to thank,
But recollected straight
    He'd business at the Bank.

                    W. S. Gilbert

Sir Galahad

My good blade carves the casques of men,
    My tough lance thrusteth sure,
My strength is as the strength of ten,
    Because my heart is pure.
The shattering trumpet shrilleth high,
    The hard brands shiver on the steel,
The splintered spear shafts crack and fly,
    The horse and rider reel:
They reel, they roll in clanging lists,
    And when the tide of combat stands,
Perfume and flowers fall in showers,
    That lightly rain from ladies' hands.

How sweet are looks that ladies bend
    On whom their favors fall!
For them I battle till the end,
    To save from shame and thrall:
But all my heart is drawn above,
    My knees are bowed in crypt and shrine:

I never felt the kiss of love,
    Nor maiden's hand in mine.
More bounteous aspects on me beam,
    Me mightier transports move and thrill;
So keep I fair through faith and prayer
    A virgin heart in work and will.

When down the stormy crescent goes,
    A light before me swims,
Between dark stems the forest glows,
    I hear a noise of hymns:
Then by some secret shrine I ride;
    I hear a voice but none are there;
The stalls are void, the doors are wide,
    The tapers burning fair.
Fair gleams the snowy altar cloth,
    The silver vessels sparkle clean,
The shrill bell rings, the censer swings,
    And solemn chants resound between.

Sometimes on lonely mountain meres
    I find a magic bark;
I leap on board: no helmsman steers:
    I float till all is dark.
A gentle sound, an awful light!
    Three angels bear the holy Grail:
With folded feet, in stoles of white,
    On sleeping wings they sail.
Ah, blessed vision! blood of God!
    My spirit beats her mortal bars,
As down dark tides the glory slides,
    And starlike mingles with the stars.

When on my goodly charger borne
    Through dreaming towns I go,

The cock crows ere the Christmas morn,
    The streets are dumb with snow.
The tempest crackles on the leads,
    And, ringing, springs from brand and mail;
But o'er the dark a glory spreads,
    And gilds the driving hail.
I leave the plain, I climb the height;
    No branchy thicket shelter yields;
But blessed forms in whistling storms
    Fly o'er waste fens and windy fields.

                    Alfred, Lord Tennyson

Sir Eglamour

Sir Eglamour, that worthy knight,
He took his sword and went to fight;
And as he rode both hill and dale,
Armèd upon his shirt of mail
A dragon came out of his den,
Had slain, God knows how many men!

When he espied Sir Eglamour,
Oh, if you had but heard him roar,
And seen how all the trees did shake,
The knight did tremble, horse did quake,
The birds betake them all to peeping—
It would have made you fall a-weeping!

But now it is in vain to fear,
Being come unto, "Fight dog! Fight bear!"
To it they go and fiercely fight
A livelong day from morn till night.

80

The dragon had a plaguey hide,
And could the sharpest steel abide.

No sword will enter him with cuts,
Which vexed the knight unto the guts;
But, as in choler he did burn,
He watched the dragon a good turn;
And, as a-yawning he did fall,
He thrust his sword in, hilts and all.

Then, like a coward, he to fly
Unto his den that was hard by;
And there he lay all night and roared.
The knight was sorry for his sword,
But, riding thence, said, "I forsake it,
He that will fetch it, let him take it!"

Samuel Rowlands

Ballade

From *Cyrano de Bergerac*

My hat is flung swiftly away;
My cloak is thrown off, if you please;
And my sword, always eager to play,
Flies out of the scabbard I seize.
My sword, I confess, is a tease,
With a nimble and mischievous brain;
And it knows, as the blade makes a breeze,
I shall strike as I end the refrain.

You should have kept quiet today.
I could carve you, my friend, by degrees.
But where? For a start, shall we say

In the side? Or the narrowest squeeze
'Twixt your ribs, while your arteries freeze,
And my point makes a sly meaning plain?
Guard that paunch! You're beginning to wheeze!
I shall strike as I end the refrain.

I need a word rhyming with *a*,
For, look, you turn paler than cheese
And whiter than—there's the word!—clay.
Your weak thrusts I parry with ease;
Too late now to pause or appease.
Hold on to your spit, though in pain,
For—if you'll permit the reprise—
I shall strike as I end the refrain.

Pray God, prince, to pardon all these
Poor efforts of yours, all in vain.
I thrust as you sink to your knees;
And I strike—as I end the refrain!

Edmond Rostand
Translated by Louis Untermeyer

Saint George and the Dragon

Saint George he slew the dragon,
   But he didn't shout hurray.
He dumped it in the wagon
   Just to clear the mess away.

But the wagoner he sold it
   To a showman at the fair
And when Saint George was told it,
   He was almost in despair.

For the people crowded round it
   To admire its teeth and claws,
But Saint George he was an Englishman
   And did not like applause.

"The creechah weighed a ton at most,"
   He muttered through his vizahd;
"I do not feel inclined to boast
   About that puny lizahd."

               Alfred Noyes

KILLERS

Danny Deever

"What are the bugles blowin' for?" said Files-on-Parade.
"To turn you out, to turn you out," the Colour-Sergeant
  said.
"What makes you look so white, so white?" said Files-on-
  Parade.
"I'm dreadin' what I've got to watch," the Colour-Sergeant
  said.
  For they're hangin' Danny Deever, you can hear the
    Dead March play,
  The regiment's in 'ollow square—they're hangin' him
    today;
  They've taken of his buttons off an' cut his stripes away,
  An' they're hangin' Danny Deever in the mornin'.

"What makes the rear-rank breathe so 'ard?" said Files-on-
  Parade.
"It's bitter cold, it's bitter cold," the Colour-Sergeant said.
"What makes that front-rank man fall down?" says Files-
  on-Parade.
"A touch o' sun, a touch o' sun," the Colour-Sergeant said.
  They are hangin' Danny Deever, they are marching of
    'im round,
  They 'ave 'alted Danny Deever by 'is coffin on the ground;
  An' 'e'll swing in 'arf a minute for a sneakin' shootin'
    hound—
  O they're hangin' Danny Deever in the mornin'.

" 'Is cot was right-'and cot to mine," said Files-on-Parade.
" 'E's sleepin' out and far tonight," the Colour-Sergeant
  said.
"I've drunk 'is beer a score o' times," said Files-on-Parade.
" 'E's drinkin' bitter beer alone," the Colour-Sergeant said.
   They are hangin' Danny Deever, you must mark 'im to
     'is place,
   For 'e shot a comrade sleeping'—you must look 'im in
     the face;
   Nine 'undred of 'is country an' the regiment's disgrace,
   While they're hangin' Danny Deever in the mornin'.

"What's that so black agin the sun?" said Files-on-Parade.
"It's Danny fightin' 'ard for life," the Colour-Sergeant said.
"What's that that whimpers over'ead?" said Files-on-Parade.
"It's Danny's soul that's passin' now," the Colour-Sergeant
  said.
   For they're done with Danny Deever, you can 'ear the
     quickstep play,
   The regiment's in column, an' they're marchin' us away;
   Ho! the young recruits are shakin' an' they'll want their
     beer today
   After hangin' Danny Deever in the mornin'.

Rudyard Kipling

The Man Hunt

The woods stretch wild to the mountain side,
And the brush is deep where a man may hide.

They have brought the bloodhounds up again
To the roadside rock where they found the slain.

They have brought the bloodhounds up, and they
Have taken the trail to the mountain way.

Three times they circled the trail and crossed,
And thrice they found it and thrice they lost.

Now straight through the pines and the underbrush
They follow the scent through the forest's hush.

And their deep-mouthed bay is a pulse of fear
In the heart of the wood that the man must hear.

The man who crouches among the trees
From the stern-faced men that follow these.

A huddle of rocks that the ooze has mossed—
And the trail of the hunted again is lost.

An upturned pebble; a bit of ground
A heel has trampled—the trail is found.

And the woods re-echo the bloodhounds' bay
As again they take to the mountain way.

A rock; a ribbon of road; a ledge,
With a pine tree clutching its crumbling edge.

A pine, that the lightning long since clave,
Whose huge roots hollow a ragged cave.

A shout; a curse; and a face aghast,
And the human quarry is laired at last.

The human quarry, with clay-clogged hair
And eyes of terror, who waits them there;

That glares and crouches and rising then
Hurls clods and curses at dogs and men.

Until the blow of a gun butt lays
Him stunned and bleeding upon his face.

A rope, a prayer, and an oak tree near,
And a score of hands to swing him clear.

A grim black thing for the setting sun
And the moon and the stars to look upon.

Madison Cawein

The Knifesmith

I am the man who made the knife
   That killed the king of Babylon;
It had a sheath of beaten gold,
   And in its haft strange jewels shone.

I wrought it through the winter days,
   And when they brightened into spring
I held it to the light, and knew
   It was a dagger for a king.

I sent it humbly to the king,
   As being fit for him to wear;
His page boy brought it back to me:
   "The king has daggers and to spare."

But while I dozed beside my fire,
   Beside my fire, as night drew on,

A hand came rustling through the wall
　　And seized the dagger and was gone.

Next morning when the king was dead,
　　And princes snarling in his hall,
The dagger he had scorned to wear
　　Was back upon my workshop wall.

And seeing it upon my wall,
　　And knowing that the king was dead,
How could I turn to making knives
　　For chopping meat or cutting bread?

No, I shall wear it at my side,
　　And wander through the world, until
On some auspicious night, we find
　　Another king for it to kill.

Dorothy Howard

Chicago Idyll

A knife within his hand he stood
　　And struck his blow by rote:
All day, for six days in the week,
　　He waded blood, and smote
Again . . . again . . . his knife into
　　A tied hog's squealing throat.

Bare to the waist, with clot and clog
　　Of steaming sweat and blood,
He watched the line of chain-caught hogs
　　Flow by in screaming flood;
And slit their red life out, that caked
　　His shoes like crimson mud.

Strange flies within an iron web,
   The writhing hogs clicked by—
One after one, in clockwork hell,
   Across a plaster sky—
Their bloodshot, little, bulging eyes
   Aware that they must die.

One hind leg noosed within a loop
   Of chain, head down they hung;
They writhed and squealed, they squealed and writhed,
   As down the room they swung,
Their damp snouts wrinkling at the smell
   Of blood from slit throats flung . . .

Of blood from throats wherein he thrust
   His blade like frozen fire . . .
He slit the soft and heavy flesh
   All day, and did not tire—
A wooden executioner
   Whose arms were twitched by wire.

He thrust the blade into their flesh
   And when he drew it out
The life came with it, choked and thick
   As from a gutterspout;
Screams spattered into gasps, his hands
   Were red with froth and gout . . .

Thus for ten bloody years he stood
   And slaughtered hogs by rote:
Ten years—ten crimson stolid years—

He waded blood, and smote
(Each day for six days in the week)
    His blade into a throat.

                *   *   *

And then one day a something clicked
    Within his heavy brain:
The Life that is not a machine,
    From every sullen vein
And artery, rose to wreak abroad
    On others its own pain.

The clockwork nightmare flood of hogs
    Still clicked its shrieking way;
The river of blood dashed on the stones
    Its steaming froth and spray:
The slaughtering went on, but he
    Took ghastly holiday.

He stood beside a struggling hog—
    His knife was at its neck;
But there the razor-whetted blade
    Found strange and sudden check;
And the tied hog went squealing by,
    Its throat without a fleck.

He stood, the knife within his hand,
    He stood and seemed to brood;
And then he turned—still knife in hand—
    From death's mere interlude . . .
And his knife (still hot with blood of hogs)
    Found fit vicissitude.

He thrust it with a practiced ease
   And a swift blow's soft jar
Straight through a fellow workman's throat
   And slit the jugular
And watched him sob his red life out
   In ways familiar.

Then knife in hand he ran amok . . . .
   Slit, slit . . . before they knew,
Men felt the hot steel in their flesh,
   And then the blood was through . . .
And then they stiffened on the floor—
   Heads hideously askew . . . .

Before the dazed and cursing men
   Could scatter from his rush,
He struck three times and from three throats
   He saw the hot life gush . . .
And then an ax beat in his skull
   Against the brain's gray plush . . . .

Even in that place of blood and doom,
   Where death was a cliché,
Men turned aside—and "Jesus Christ!"
   Was all that they could say.
And then the hogs moved on once more
   Upon their screaming way.

E. Merrill Root

The Wolves

Last night knives flashed. LeChien cried
And chewed blood in his bed.
Vanni's whittling blade
Had found flesh easier than wood.

Vanni and I left camp on foot. In a glade
We came on a brown blossom
Great and shining on a thorned stem.
"That's the sensitive brier," I said.

"It shrinks at the touch," I added.
Soon we found buffalo. Picking
A bull grazing by itself, I began
The approach: while the shaggy head

Was turned I sprinted across the sod,
And when he swung around his gaze
I bellyflopped in the grass
And lay on my heartbeat and waited.

When he looked away again I made
Enough yardage before he wheeled
His head: I kneeled, leveled
My rifle, and we calmly waited.

It occurred to me as we waited
That in those last moments he was,
In fact, daydreaming about something else.
"He is too stupid to live," I said.

His legs shifted and the heart showed.
I fired. He looked, trotted off,
He simply looked and trotted off,
Stumbled, sat himself down, and became dead.

I looked for Vanni. Amid the cows he stood,
Only his arms moving as he fired,
Loaded, and fired, the dumb herd
Milling about him sniffing at their dead.

I called and he retreated.
We cut two choice tongues for ourselves
And left the surplus. All day wolves
Would splash blood from those great sides.

Again we saw the flower, brown-red
On a thorn-spiked stem. When Vanni
Extended his fingers, it was funny,
It shrank away as if it had just died.

They told us in camp that LeChien was dead.
None of us cared. Nobody much
Had liked him. His tobacco pouch,
I observed, was already missing from beside his bed.

Galway Kinnell

Camp Fever

Camped by a creek and didn't speak for a week:
The continual bell of the smaller frogs, the croak
Of "bulls" in the bulrushes, and the chirp
Of crickets in my bunk. He'd harp and harp,

That fellow, on the weather, until, I tell you,
I, maddened, could but threaten, "Very well, you—"
And then we two fell out, fell on each other,
And bitterly fought as brother fights with brother.
A bloody mess, the tent, and out he went,
His two lights out; fell into the river. Meant
To bathe his wounds; wound up instead
As posted missing in the flood. Poor dead
Cow, now, I miss him. Now I tramp the river;
How I'd nurse him, to drag him out and shiver
Listening to his tales of weather, never
Again to quarrel, or pitch in peril of camp fever.

John Blight

The Hunter

I have fought against the poodle with his gory, deadly
    paws;
I have faced the fearsome kitten, wild and bony,
And somehow I have evaded the enormous chomping jaws
Of the frighteningly ferocious Shetland pony.

My triumph o'er the rabbit now is sung throughout the
    land,
And men still speak in whispers of the day
When, attacked by twelve mosquitoes, with my one
    unwounded hand,
I killed nine of them and drove the rest away.

I have faced the housefly in his lair, I've stalked the ladybug
And the caterpillar, grim and fierce and hairy;
That trophy there is bumblebee, and this, my favorite rug,
Has been fashioned from the hide of a canary.

I have dove into the ocean to do combat with a shrimp,
I have dared the hen to come on out and fight;
I have battled with the butterfly (that's why I have this
    limp),
And I slewed a monstrous grubworm just last night.

But this evening I must sally forth to meet the savage moth,
And if I don't come back in time for tea,
You shall know that I fell gallantly, as gallantly I fought
So please be gentle when you speak of me.

Shel Silverstein

Samuel Hall

My name is Samuel Hall, Samuel Hall,
My name is Samuel Hall, and I hate you one and all;
    You're a gang of muckers all—
        Damn your eyes!

O, I killed a man 'tis said, so 'tis said,
O, I killed a man 'tis said and I smashed his bleeding head,
    And I left him lying dead—
        Damn his eyes!

So they put me into quod, into quod,
So they put me into quod with a bar and iron rod,
    And they left me there, by God—
        Damn their eyes!

O, the parson he did come, he did come,
O, the parson he did come and he looked so very glum

As he talked of kingdom come—
　　Damn his eyes!

O, the sheriff he came too, he came too,
O, the sheriff he came too, with his little boys in blue
　　Saying, "Sam, I'll see you through"—
　　Damn his eyes!

I saw Nellie in the crowd, in the crowd,
I saw Nellie in the crowd and I shouted right out loud,
　　"Say, Nellie, ain't you proud?"—
　　Damn your eyes!

So a swinging up I'll go, up I'll go,
So a swinging up I'll go while you people down below
　　Shout up, "Sam, I told you so."—
　　Damn your eyes!

American folk ballad

Jack Hall

My name it is Jack Hall, chimney sweep, chimney sweep,
My name it is Jack Hall, chimney sweep.
My name it is Jack Hall and I'll rob both great and small,
My neck shall pay for all when I die, when I die,
My neck shall pay for all when I die.

I've twenty cows in store, that's no joke, that's no joke,
I've twenty cows in store, that's no joke.
I've twenty cows in store and I'll rob for twenty more,
My neck shall pay for all when I die, when I die,
My neck shall pay for all when I die.

I've candles lily white, that's no joke, that's no joke,
I've candles lily white, that's no joke.
I've candles lily white, O I stole them in the night
For to light me to the place where I lie, where I lie,
For to light me to the place where I lie.

They tell me that in jail I shall die, I shall die,
They tell me that in jail I shall die.
They tell me that in jail I shall drink no more brown ale
But be dashed if ever I fail till I die, till I die,
But be dashed if ever I fail till I die.

I rode up Tyburn's Hill in a cart, in a cart,
I rode up Tyburn's Hill in a cart.
I rode up Tyburn's Hill and 'twas there I made my will,
Saying the best of friends must part, so farewell, so
    farewell,
Saying the best of friends must part, so farewell.

O I climbed up the ladder, that's no joke, that's no joke,
O I climbed up the ladder, that's no joke,
O I climbed up the ladder and the hangman spread the rope,
And the devil of a word said I coming down, coming down,
And the devil of a word said I coming down.

English folk ballad

"Plot Improbable, Character Unsympathetic"

I was born in a bad slum
Where no one had to die
To show his skeleton.
The wind came through the walls,

100

A three-legged rat and I
Fought all day for swill.
My father was crazed, my mother cruel,
My brothers chopped the stairs for fuel,
I tumbled my sisters in a broken bed
And jiggled them till all were dead.
Then I ran away and lived with my lice
On my wits, a knife, and a pair of dice,
Slept like a rat in the river reeds,
Got converted fifty times
To fifty different creeds
For bowls of mission broth,
Till I killed the grocer and his wife
With a stove poker and a carving knife.
The mayor said, Hang him high,
The merchants said, He won't buy or sell,
The bishop said, He won't pay to pray.
They flung me into a jail,
But I, I broke out,
Beat my bars to a bell,
Ran all around the town
Dingling my sweet bell,
And the mayor wanted it for his hall,
The merchants wanted to buy it,
The bishop wanted it for his church,
But I broke my bell in two,
Of one half a huge bullet made,
Of the other an enormous gun,
Took all the people of all the world
And rolled them into one,
And when the World went by
With a monocle in his eye,
With a silk hat on his head,
Took aim and shot him dead.

Elder Olson

The Three Butchers

It was Ips, Gips, and Johnson, as I've heard many say,
They had five hundred guineas, all on a market day:
As they rode over Northumberland, as hard as they could
    ride,
Oh, hark, oh, hark, says Johnson, I hear a woman cry.

Then Johnson, being a valiant man, a man of courage bold,
He ranged the woods all over, till this woman he did behold.
How came you here? says Johnson, how came you here, I
    pray?
I am come to relieve you, if you will not me betray.

There have been ten swaggering blades, have hand and
    foot me bound,
And stripped me stark naked, with my hair pinned on the
    ground;
Then Johnson, being a valiant man, a man of courage bold,
He took his coat from off his back, to keep her from the cold.

As they rode over Northumberland, as hard as they could
    ride,
She put her fingers in her ears, and dismally she cried,
Then up started ten swaggering blades, with weapons in
    their hand,
And, riding up to Johnson, they bid him for to stand.

It's I'll not stand, said Ipson, then no indeed, not I,
Nor I'll not stand, said Gipson, I'd sooner live than die.
Then I will stand, said Johnson, I'll stand the while I can,
I never yet was daunted, nor afraid of any man.

Then Johnson drew his glittering sword, with all his might
and main,
So well he laid upon them, that eight of them were slain;
As he was fighting the other two, this woman he did not
mind,
She took the knife all from his side, and ripped him up
behind.

Now I must fall, says Johnson, I must fall unto the ground,
For relieving this wicked woman, she gave me my death
wound;
Oh base woman, oh base woman, whatever hast thou done,
Thou hast killed the finest butcher that ever the sun shone
on.

This happened on a market day, as people were riding by,
To see this dreadful murder, they gave the hue and cry,
It's now this woman's taken, and bound in irons strong,
For killing the finest butcher that ever the sun shone on.

Anonymous

The Spectre Pig

It was the stalwart butcher man,
    That knit his swarthy brow,
And said the gentle Pig must die,
    And sealed it with a vow.

And oh! it was the gentle Pig
    Lay stretched upon the ground,
And ah! it was the cruel knife
    His little heart that found.

They took him then, those wicked men,
  They trailed him all along:
They put a stick between his lips,
  And through his heels a thong;

And round and round an oaken beam
  A hempen cord they flung,
And, like a mighty pendulum,
  All solemnly he swung!

Now say thy prayers, thou sinful man,
  And think what thou hast done,
And read thy catechism well,
  Thou bloody-minded one;

For if his sprite should walk by night,
  It better were for thee,
That thou wert moldering in the ground,
  Or bleaching in the sea.

It was the savage butcher then,
  That made a mock of sin,
And swore a very wicked oath,
  He did not care a pin.

It was the butcher's youngest son,
  His voice was broke with sighs,
And with his pocket handkerchief
  He wiped his little eyes;

All young and ignorant was he,
  But innocent and mild,
And, in his soft simplicity,
  Out spoke the tender child:

"Oh, father, father, list to me;
    The Pig is deadly sick,
And men have hung him by his heels,
    And fed him with a stick."

It was the bloody butcher then,
    That laughed as he would die,
Yet did he soothe the sorrowing child,
    And bid him not to cry;

"Oh, Nathan, Nathan, what's a Pig,
    That thou shouldst weep and wail?
Come, bear thee like a butcher's child,
    And thou shalt have his tail!"

It was the butcher's daughter then,
    So slender and so fair,
That sobbed as if her heart would break,
    And tore her yellow hair;

And thus she spoke in thrilling tone,
    Fast fell the teardrops big:
"Ah! woe is me! Alas! Alas!
    The Pig! The Pig! The Pig!"

Then did her wicked father's lips
    Make merry with her woe,
And call her many a naughty name,
    Because she whimpered so.

Ye need not weep, ye gentle ones,
    In vain your tears are shed,
Ye cannot wash his crimson hand,
    Ye cannot soothe the dead.

The bright sun folded on his breast
  His robes of rosy flame,
And softly over all the west
  The shades of evening came.

He slept, and troops of murdered Pigs
  Were busy with his dreams;
Loud rang their wild, unearthly shrieks,
  Wide yawned their mortal seams.

*   *   *

The clock struck twelve; the Dead hath heard;
  He opened both his eyes,
And sullenly he shook his tail
  To lash the feeding flies.

One quiver of the hempen cord,
  One struggle and one bound,
With stiffened limb and leaden eye,
  The Pig was on the ground!

And straight towards the sleeper's house
  His fearful way he wended;
And hooting owl and hovering bat
  On midnight wing attended.

Back flew the bolt, up rose the latch,
  And open swung the door,
And little mincing feet were heard
  Pat, pat along the floor.

Two hoofs upon the sanded floor,
  And two upon the bed;
And they are breathing side by side,
  The living and the dead!

106

"Now wake, now wake, thou butcher man!
    What makes thy cheek so pale?
Take hold! take hold! thou dost not fear
    To clasp a spectre's tail?"

Untwisted every winding coil;
    The shuddering wretch took hold,
All like an icicle it seemed,
    So tapering and so cold.

"Thou com'st with me, thou butcher man!"
    He strives to loose his grasp,
But, faster than the clinging vine,
    Those twining spirals clasp:

And open, open swung the door,
    And, fleeter than the wind,
The shadowy spectre swept before,
    The butcher trailed behind.

Fast fled the darkness of the night,
    And morn rose faint and dim;
They called full loud, they knocked full long,
    They did not waken him.

Straight, straight towards that oaken beam,
    A trampled pathway ran;
A ghastly shape was swinging there—
    It was the butcher man.

                    Oliver Wendell Holmes

Ballad of the Long Drop

We dropped a chap that raped a child:
He gave no trouble, kind and mild.
We dropped a kid that killed a cop:
He made a lightish drop.

We dropped a well-fed man who bled
Old ladies—and the prayers he said!
We dropped a gangster who was bold
But shivered with the cold.

We dropped a gentlemanly rake
Who said it wasn't our mistake;
We dropped a fool or two who tried
To struggle as they died.

We dropped a lad who killed by whim,
Who cursed us as we pinioned him.
We dropped a girl who shot a bloke
Because her heart was broke.

Her heart was broke. She did him in
For love: but love like hers is sin.
We dropped her, for we drop them straight
For love as well as hate.

For love as well as hate we serve
To break the neck and break the nerve
Of those who break the laws of man:
We serve you all as best we can.

John Pudney

THE FIGHTING IRISH

The Fighting Race

"Read out the names!" and Burke sat back,
   And Kelly drooped his head,
While Shea—they called him Scholar Jack—
   Went down the list of the dead.
Officers, seamen, gunners, marines,
   The crews of the gig and yawl,
The bearded man and the lad in his teens,
   Carpenters, coal passers—all.
Then, knocking the ashes from out his pipe,
   Said Burke in an offhand way:
"We're all in that dead man's list, by cripe!
   Kelly and Burke and Shea."
"Well, here's to the *Maine*, and I'm sorry for Spain,"
   Said Kelly and Burke and Shea.

"Wherever there's Kellys there's trouble," said Burke.
   "Wherever fighting's the game,
Or a spice of danger in grown man's work,"
   Said Kelly, "you'll find my name."
"And do we fall short," said Burke, getting mad,
   "When it's touch and go for life?"

Said Shea, "It's thirty-odd years, bedad,
    Since I charged to drum and fife
Up Marye's Heights, and my old canteen
    Stopped a rebel ball on its way;
There were blossoms of blood on our sprigs of green—
    Kelly and Burke and Shea—
And the dead didn't brag." "Well, here's to the flag!"
    Said Kelly and Burke and Shea.

"I wish 'twas in Ireland, for there's the place,"
    Said Burke, "that we'd die by right,
In the cradle of our soldier race,
    After one good stand-up fight.
My grandfather fell on Vinegar Hill,
    And fighting was not his trade;
But his rusty pike's in the cabin still,
    With Hessian blood on the blade."
"Aye, aye," said Kelly, "the pikes were great
    When the word was 'clear the way!'
We were thick on the roll in ninety-eight—
    Kelly and Burke and Shea."
"Well, here's to the pike and the sword and the like!"
    Said Kelly and Burke and Shea.

And Shea, the scholar, with rising joy,
    Said, "We were at Ramillies;
We left our bones at Fontenoy
    And up in the Pyrenees;
Before Dunkirk, on Landen's plain,
    Cremona, Lille, and Ghent;
We're all over Austria, France and Spain,
    Wherever they pitched a tent.
We've died for England from Waterloo
    To Egypt and Dargai;

And still there's enough for a corps or crew,
   Kelly and Burke and Shea."
"Well, here's to good honest fighting blood!"
   Said Kelly and Burke and Shea.

"Oh, the fighting races don't die out,
   If they seldom die in bed,
For love is first in their hearts, no doubt,"
   Said Burke; then Kelly said:
"When Michael, the Irish Archangel, stands,
   The Angel with the sword,
And the battle dead from a hundred lands
   Are ranged in one big horde,
Our line, that for Gabriel's trumpet waits,
   Will stretch three deep that day,
From Jehoshaphat to the Golden Gates—
   Kelly and Burke and Shea."
"Well, here's thank God for the race and the sod!"
   Said Kelly and Burke and Shea.

Joseph I. C. Clarke

Mush, Mush

Oh, 'twas there I larned readin' an' writin',
At Billy Brackett's where I went to school;
And 'twas there I larned howlin' an' fightin',
Wid me schoolmaster Mister O'Toole;
We had mony a scrimmage,
And divil a copy I wrote;
There was ne'er a gossoon in the village
Dared thread on the tail o' me—
   Mush, mush, mush, tu-ral-i-addy,
   Sing mush, mush, mush, tu-ral-i-ay!

There was ne'er a gossoon in the village,
Dared thread on the tail o' me coat!

Oh, 'twas there I larned all me courtin',
Oh, the lissons I tuck in the art!
Till Cupid, the blackguard, while sportin',
An arrow dhruv straight through me heart.
Miss Judy O'Connor, she lived just forninst me,
And tinder lines to her I wrote;
If ye dare say one hard word agin her,
I'll thread on the tail o' yer—. . . *mush, mush, etc.*

But a blackguard, called Micky Maloney,
Came an' sthole her affictions away;
For he'd mony an' I hadn't ony
So I sint him a challenge nixt day.
In the A.M. we met at Killarney,
The Shannon we crossed in a boat;
An' I lathered him wid me shillaly,
For he throd on the tail o' me— . . . *mush, mush, etc.*

Oh, me fame wint abroad through the nation,
An' folks came a-flockin' to see;
An' they cried out widout hesitation:
"You're a fightin' man, Billy McGee!"
Oh, I've claned up the Finnigan faction,
An' I've licked all the Murphys afloat;
If you're in fur a row or a raction,
Jist ye thread on the tail o' me—
  Mush, mush, mush, tu-ral-i-addy,
  Mush, mush, mush, tu-ral-i-ay!
If you're in fer a row or a raction,
Jist ye thread on the tail o' me coat!

Irish music-hall song

114

Arthur McBride

I once knew a fellow named Arthur McBride,
And he and I rambled down by the seaside,
A-looking for pleasure or what might betide,
And the weather was pleasant and charming.

So gaily and gallant we went on our tramp,
And we met Sergeant Harper and Corporal Cramp,
And the little wee fellow who roused up the camp
With his row-de-dow-dow in the morning.

"Good morning, young fellows," the sergeant he cried.
"And the same to you, sergeant," was all our reply.
There was nothing more spoken; we made to pass by
And continue our walk in the morning.

"Well now, my fine fellows, if you will enlist,
A guinea in gold I will slap in your fist,
And a crown in the bargain to kick up the dust
And drink the Queen's health in the morning."

"O no, mister sergeant, we aren't for sale.
We'll make no such bargain, and your bribe won't avail.
We're not tired of our country, and don't care to sail,
Though your offer is pleasant and charming.

If we were such fools as to take your advance,
It's right bloody slender would be our poor chance,
For the Queen wouldn't scruple to send us to France
And get us all shot in the morning."

"Ha now, you young blackguards, if you say one more
    word,
I swear by the herrins, I'll draw out my sword
And run through your bodies as my strength may afford;
So now, you young buggers, take warning!"

Well, we beat that bold drummer as flat as a shoe,
And we make a football of his row-de-dow-do,
And as for the others, we knocked out the two.
Oh, we were the boys in that morning!

We took the old weapons that hung by their side
And flung them as far as we could in the tide.
"May the devil go with you," says Arthur McBride,
"For delaying our walk this fine morning!"

Irish folk song

The Irishman and the Lady

There was a lady lived at Leith,
    A lady very stylish, man;
And yet, in spite of all her teeth,
    She fell in love with an Irishman—
        A nasty, ugly Irishman,
        A wild, tremendous Irishman,
A tearing, swearing, thumping, bumping, ranting, roaring
    Irishman.

His face was no ways beautiful,
    For with smallpox 'twas scarred across;
And the shoulders of the ugly dog
    Were almost double a yard across.

116

Oh, the lump of an Irishman,
The whiskey-devouring Irishman,
The great he-rogue with his wonderful brogue—the
fighting, rioting Irishman.

One of his eyes was bottle-green,
And the other eye was out, my dear;
And the calves of his wicked-looking legs
Were more than two feet about, my dear.
Oh, the great big Irishman,
The rattling, battling Irishman—
The stamping, ramping, swaggering, staggering, leathering
swash of an Irishman.

He took so much of lundyfoot [1]
That he used to snort and snuffle—O!
And in shape and size the fellow's neck
Was as bad as the neck of a buffalo.
Oh, the horrible Irishman,
The thundering, blundering Irishman—
The slashing, dashing, smashing, lashing, thrashing,
hashing Irishman.

His name was a terrible name, indeed,
Being Timothy Thady Mulligan;
And whenever he emptied his tumbler of punch
He'd not rest till he filled it full again.
The boozing, bruising Irishman,
The 'toxicated Irishman—
The whiskey, frisky, rummy, gummy, brandy, no dandy
Irishman.

[1] lundyfoot: a kind of snuff

This was the lad the lady loved,
    Like all the girls of quality;
And he broke the skulls of the men of Leith,
    Just by the way of jollity.
        Oh, the leathering Irishman,
        The barbarous, savage Irishman—
The hearts of the maids, and the gentlemen's heads, were
    bothered I'm sure by this Irishman.

                                        William Maginn

Paddy Murphy

The night that Paddy Murphy died
I never shall forget!
The whole damn town got stinking drunk
And they're not sober yet.

There is one thing they did that night
That filled me full of fear:
They took the ice right off the corpse
And stuck it in the beer.

That's how they showed their respect for Paddy Murphy,
That's how they showed their honor and their fight,
That's how they showed their respect for Paddy Murphy;
They drank his health in ice-cold beer that night!

                                        Anonymous

Dooley Is a Traitor

"So then you won't fight?"
"Yes, your Honor," I said, "that's right."
"Now is it that you simply aren't willing,
Or have you a fundamental moral objection to killing?"
Says the judge, blowing his nose
And making his words stand to attention in long rows.
I stand to attention too, but with half a grin
(In my time I've done a good many in).
"No objection at all, sir," I said.
"There's a deal of the world I'd rather see dead—
Such as Johnny Stubbs or Fred Settle or my last landlord,
    Mr. Syme.
Give me a gun and your blessing, your Honor, and I'll be
    killing them all the time.
But my conscience says a clear no
To killing a crowd of gentlemen I don't know.
Why, I'd as soon think of killing a worshipful judge,
High-court, like yourself (against whom, God knows, I've
    got no grudge—
So far), as murder a heap of foreign folk.
If you've got no grudge, you've got no joke
To laugh at after."
                  Now the words never come flowing
Proper for me till I get the old pipe going.
And just as I was poking
Down baccy, the judge looks up sharp with "No smoking,
Mr. Dooley. We're not fighting this war for fun.
And we want a clearer reason why you refuse to carry a
    gun.
This war is not a personal feud, it's a fight
Against wrong ideas on behalf of the Right.

Mr. Dooley, won't you help to destroy evil ideas?"
"Ah, your Honor, here's
The tragedy," I said. "I'm not a man of the mind.
I couldn't find it in my heart to be unkind
To an idea. I wouldn't know one if I saw one. I haven't one
  of my own.
So I'd best be leaving other people's alone."
"Indeed," he sneers at me, "this defense is
Curious for someone with convictions in two senses.
A criminal invokes conscience to his aid
To support an individual withdrawal from a communal
  crusade
Sanctioned by God, led by the Church, against a godless,
  churchless nation!"
I asked his Honor for a translation.
"You talk of conscience," he said. "What do you know of
  the Christian Creed?"
"Nothing, sir, except what I can read.
That's the most you can hope for from us jailbirds.
I just open the book here and there and look at the words.
And I find when the Lord himself misliked an evil notion
He turned it into a pig and drove it squealing over a cliff
  into the ocean,
And the loony ran away
And lived to think another day.
There was a clean job done and no blood shed!
Everybody happy and forty wicked thoughts drowned
  dead.
A neat and Christian murder. None of your mad slaughter
Throwing away the brains with the blood and the baby
  with the bath water.
Now I look at the war as a sportsman. It's a matter of
  choosing
The decentest way of losing.

Heads or tails, losers or winners,
We all lose, we're all damned sinners.
And I'd rather be with the poor cold people at the wall
that's shot
Than the bloody guilty devils in the firing line, in Hell and
keeping hot."
"But what right, Dooley, what right," he cried,
"Have you to say the Lord is on your side?"
"That's a dirty crooked question," back I roared.
"I said not the Lord was on my side, but I was on the side
of the Lord."
Then he was up at me and shouting,
But by and by he calms: "Now we're not doubting
Your sincerity, Dooley, only your arguments,
Which don't make sense."
("Hullo," I thought, "that's the wrong way round.
I may be skylarking a bit, but my brainpan's sound.")
Then biting his nail and sugaring his words sweet:
"Keep your head, Mr. Dooley. Religion is clearly not up
your street.
But let me ask you as a plain patriotic fellow
Whether you'd stand there so smug and yellow
If the foe were attacking your own dear sister."
"I'd knock their brains out, mister,
On the floor," I said. "There," he says kindly, "I knew you
were no pacifist.
It's your straight duty as a man to enlist.
The enemy is at the door." You could have downed
Me with a feather. "Where?" I gasp, looking round.
"Not this door," he says, angered. "Don't play the clown.
But they're two thousand miles away planning to do us
down.
Why, the news is full of the deeds of those murderers and
rapers."

"Your Eminence," I said, "my father told me never to
   believe the papers
But to go by my eyes,
And at two thousand miles the poor things can't tell truth
   from lies."
His fearful spectacles glittered like the moon: "For the last
   time what right
Has a man like you to refuse to fight?"
"More right," I said, "than you.
You've never murdered a man, so you don't know what it
   is I won't do.
I've done it in good hot blood, so haven't I the right to
   make bold
To declare that I shan't do it in cold?"
Then the judge rises in a great rage
And writes *Dooley Is a Traitor* in black upon a page
And tells me I must die.
"What, me?" says I.
"If you still won't fight."
"Well, yes, your Honor," I said, "that's right."

                                                  James Michie

Bold O'Donahue

Well here I am from Paddy's land, a land of high renown,
I broke the hearts of all the girls for miles 'round Keady
   Town.
And when they hear that I'm awa' they'll raise a
   hullabaloo,
When they hear about that handsome lad they call
   O'Donahue.

122

Chorus:

*For I'm the boy to please her and I'm the boy to tease
her,*
*I'm the boy can squeeze her, och! and I'll tell you what
I'll do.*
*I'll court her like an Irishman, and the brogue and
blarney too is my plan,*
*With the rolligan, swolligan, holligan, wolligan, Bold
O'Donahue!*

I wish my love was a red, red rose growing on yon garden
wall,
And me to be a drewdrop and upon her brow I'd fall;
Perhaps now she might think of me as a rather heavy
dew,
And no more she'd love that handsome lad they call
O'Donahue!

Well I hear that Queen Victoria has a daughter fine and
grand,
Perhaps she'd take it into her head for to marry an
Irishman;
And if only I could get the chance to have a word or two,
I'm sure she'd take a notion in the Bold O'Donahue.

Irish folk song

Danny

One night a score of Erris men,
A score I'm told and nine,
Said, "We'll get shut of Danny's noise
Of girls and widows dyin'.

"There's not his like from Binghamstown
To Boyle and Ballycroy,
At playing hell on decent girls,
At beating man and boy.

"He's left two pairs of female twins
Beyond in Killacreest,
And twice in Crossmolina fair
He's struck the parish priest.

"But we'll come round him in the night
A mile beyond the Mullet;
Ten will quench his bloody eyes,
And ten will choke his gullet."

It wasn't long till Danny came,
From Bangor making way,
And he was damning moon and stars
And whistling grand and gay.

Till in a gap of hazel glen—
And not a hare in sight—
Out lepped the nine-and-twenty lads
Along his left and right.

Then Danny smashed the nose on Byrne,
He split the lips on three,
And bit across the right-hand thumb
On one Red Shawn Magee.

But seven tripped him up behind,
And seven kicked before,
And seven squeezed around his throat
Till Danny kicked no more.

Then some destroyed him with their heels,
Some tramped him in the mud,
Some stole his purse and timber pipe,
And some washed off his blood.

And when you're walking out the way
From Bangor to Belmullet,
You'll see a flat cross on a stone,
Where men choked Danny's gullet.

John Millington Synge

Drill, Ye Tarriers, Drill

Every morning at seven o'clock
There were twenty tarriers a-working on the rock,
And the boss comes along and he says, "Keep still,
And come down heavy on the cast-iron drill!"

Chorus:
And drill, ye tarriers, drill!
Drill, ye tarriers, drill!

Oh, it's work all day
For the sugar in your tay
Down behind the railway,
Drill, ye tarriers, drill!
And blast! and fire!

The boss was a fine man down to the ground
And he married a lady six feet 'round;
She baked good bread, and she baked it well,
But she baked it hard as the holes in hell!

Now the new foreman was Jean McCann;
By God, he was a blamed mean man!
Last week a premature blast went off,
And a mile in the air went big Jim Goff.

The next time pay day came around,
Jim Goff a dollar short was found.
When he asked what for, came this reply:
"You were docked for the time you were up in the sky."

Thomas F. Casey

126

IN FARAWAY PLACES

The Shooting of Dan McGrew

A bunch of the boys were whooping it up in the Malamute
saloon;
The kid that handles the music box was hitting a jag-time
tune;
Back of the bar, in a solo game, sat Dangerous Dan
McGrew,
And watching his luck was his light-o'-love, the lady that's
known as Lou.

When out of the night, which was fifty below, and into the
din and the glare,
There stumbled a miner fresh from the creeks, dog-dirty,
and loaded for bear.
He looked like a man with a foot in the grave and scarcely
the strength of a louse,
Yet he tilted a poke of dust on the bar, and he called for
drinks for the house.
There was none could place the stranger's face, though we
searched ourselves for a clue;
But we drank his health, and the last to drink was
Dangerous Dan McGrew.

There's men that somehow just grip your eyes, and hold
  them hard like a spell;
And such was he, and he looked to me like a man who had
  lived in hell;
With a face most hair, and the dreary stare of a dog whose
  day is done,
As he watered the green stuff in his glass, and the drops
  fell one by one.
Then I got to figgering who he was, and wondering what
  he'd do,
And I turned my head—and there watching him was the
  lady that's known as Lou.

His eyes went rubbering round the room, and he seemed in
  a kind of daze,
Till at last that old piano fell in the way of his wandering
  gaze.
The ragtime kid was having a drink; there was no one else
  on the stool,
So the stranger stumbles across the room, and flops down
  there like a fool.
In a buckskin shirt that was glazed with dirt he sat, and I
  saw him sway;
Then he clutched the keys with his talon hands—my God!
  but that man could play.

Were you ever out in the Great Alone, when the moon was
  awful clear,
And the icy mountains hemmed you in with a silence you
  'most could *hear;*
With only the howl of a timber wolf, and you camped there
  in the cold,
A half-dead thing in a stark, dead world, clean mad for the
  muck called gold;
While high overhead, green, yellow and red, the North
  Lights swept in bars?—

Then you've a hunch what the music meant . . . hunger
    and night and the stars.

And hunger not of the belly kind, that's banished with
    bacon and beans,
But the gnawing hunger of lonely men for a home and all
    that it means;
For a fireside far from the cares that are, four walls and a
    roof above;
But oh! so cram-full of cozy joy, and crowned with a
    woman's love—
A woman dearer than all the world, and true as Heaven is
    true—
(God! how ghastly she looks through her rouge—the lady
    that's known as Lou.)

Then on a sudden the music changed, so soft that you
    scarce could hear;
But you felt that your life had been looted clean of all that
    it once held dear;
That someone had stolen the woman you loved; that her
    love was a devil's lie;
That your guts were gone, and the best for you was to
    crawl away and die.
'Twas the crowning cry of a heart's despair, and it thrilled
    you through and through—
"I guess I'll make it a spread misère," said Dangerous Dan
    McGrew.

The music almost died away . . . then it burst like a
    pent-up flood;
And it seemed to say, "Repay, repay," and my eyes were
    blind with blood.
The thought came back of an ancient wrong, and it stung
    like a frozen lash,

And the lust awoke to kill, to kill . . . then the music
    stopped with a crash,
And the stranger turned, and his eyes they burned in a
    most peculiar way;

In a buckskin shirt that was glazed with dirt he sat, and I
    saw him sway;
Then his lips went in in a kind of grin, and he spoke, and
    his voice was calm,
And "Boys," says he, "you don't know me, and none of
    you care a damn;
But I want to state, and my words are straight, and I'll bet
    my poke they're true,
That one of you is a hound of hell . . . and that one is
    Dan McGrew."

Then I ducked my head, and the lights went out, and two
    guns blazed in the dark,
And a woman screamed, and the lights went up, and two
    men lay stiff and stark.
Pitched on his head, and pumped full of lead, was
    Dangerous Dan McGrew,
While the man from the creeks lay clutched to the breast
    of the lady that's known as Lou.

These are the simple facts of the case, and I guess I ought
    to know.
They say that the stranger was crazed with "hooch," and
    I'm not denying it's so.
I'm not so wise as the lawyer guys, but strictly between us
    two—
The woman that kissed him and—pinched his poke—was
    the lady that's known as Lou.

Robert W. Service

132

The Ballad of Yukon Jake

Begging Robert W. Service's Pardon

Oh the North Countree is a hard countree
That mothers a bloody brood;
And its icy arms hold hidden charms
For the greedy, the sinful and lewd.
And strong men rust, from the gold and the lust
That sears the Northland soul,
But the wickedest born, from the Pole to the Horn,
Is the Hermit of Shark Tooth Shoal.

Now Jacob Kaime was the Hermit's name
In the days of his pious youth,
Ere he cast a smirch on the Baptist Church
By betraying a girl named Ruth.
But now men quake at "Yukon Jake,"
The Hermit of Shark Tooth Shoal,
For that is the name that Jacob Kaime
Is known by from Nome to the Pole.
He was just a boy and the parson's joy
(Ere he fell for the gold and the muck),
And had learned to pray, with the hogs and the hay
On a farm near Keokuk.
But a Service tale of illicit kale,
And whisky and women wild,
Drained the morals clean as a soup tureen
From this poor but honest child.
He longed for the bite of a Yukon night
And the Northern Light's weird flicker,
Or a game of stud in the frozen mud,
And the taste of raw red licker.

133

He wanted to mush along in the slush,
With a team of husky hounds,
And to fire his gat at a beaver hat
And knock it out of bounds.

So he left his home for the hell-town Nome,
On Alaska's ice-ribbed shores,
And he learned to curse and to drink, and worse,
Till the rum dripped from his pores.
When the boys on a spree were drinking it free
In a Malamute saloon
And Dan Megrew and his dangerous crew
Shot craps to the crazy tune,
As the Kid on his stool banged away like a fool
At a jag-time melody,
And the barkeep vowed, to the hard-boiled crowd,
That he'd cree-mate Sam McGee—

Then Jacob Kaime, who had taken the name
Of Yukon Jake, the Killer,
Would rake the dive with his forty-five
Till the atmosphere grew chiller.
With a sharp command he'd make 'em stand
And deliver their hard-earned dust,
Then drink the bar dry of rum and rye,
As a Klondike bully must.
Without coming to blows he would tweak the nose
Of Dangerous Dan Megrew,
And, becoming bolder, throw over his shoulder
The lady that's known as Lou.
Oh, tough as a steak was Yukon Jake—
Hard-boiled as a picnic egg.
He washed his shirt in the Klondike dirt,
And drank his rum by the keg.

In fear of their lives (or because of their wives)
He was shunned by the best of his pals,
An outcast he, from the comradery
Of all but wild animals.
So he bought him the whole of Shark Tooth Shoal,
A reef in the Bering Sea,
And he lived by himself on a sea lion's shelf
In lonely iniquity.

But, miles away, in Keokuk, Ia.,
Did a ruined maiden fight
To remove the smirch from the Baptist Church
By bringing the heathen Light;
And the Elders declared that all would be spared
If she carried the holy words
From her Keokuk home to the hell-town Nome
To save those sinful birds.

So, two weeks later, she took a freighter,
For the gold-cursed land near the Pole,
But Heaven ain't made for a lass that's betrayed—
She was wrecked on Shark Tooth Shoal!
All hands were tossed in the sea, and lost—
All but the maiden Ruth,
Who swam to the edge of the sea lion's ledge
Where abode the love of her youth.
He was hunting a seal for his evening meal
(He handled a mean harpoon)
When he saw at his feet, not something to eat,
But a girl in a frozen swoon,
Whom he dragged to his lair by her dripping hair,
And he rubbed her knees with gin.
To his great surprise, she opened her eyes
And revealed—his Original Sin!

His eight-month beard grew stiff and weird,
And it felt like a chestnut burr,
And he swore by his gizzard and the Arctic blizzard
That he'd do right by her.
But the cold sweat froze on the end of her nose
Till it gleamed like a Tecla pearl,
While her bright hair fell, like a flame from hell,
Down the back of the grateful girl.
But a hopeless rake was Yukon Jake,
The hermit of Shark Tooth Shoal!
And the dizzy maid he rebetrayed
And wrecked her immortal soul! . . .
Then he rowed her ashore, with a broken oar,
And he sold her to Dan Megrew
For a husky dog and some hot eggnog,
As rascals are wont to do.
Now ruthless Ruth is a maid uncouth
With scarlet cheeks and lips,
And she sings rough songs to the drunken throngs
That come from the sealing ships.
For a rouge-stained kiss from this infamous miss
They will give a seal's sleek fur,
Or perhaps a sable, if they are able;
It's much the same to her.

Oh, the North Countree is a rough countree,
That mothers a bloody brood;
And its icy arms hold hidden charms
For the greedy, the sinful and lewd.
And strong men rust, from the gold and the lust
That sears the Northland soul,
But the wickedest born from the Pole to the Horn
Was the Hermit of Shark Tooth Shoal!

Edward E. Paramore, Jr.

My Friends

The man above was a murderer, the man below was a
    thief;
And I lay there in the bunk between, ailing beyond belief;
A weary armful of skin and bone, wasted with pain and
    grief.

My feet were froze, and the lifeless toes were purple and
    green and gray;
The little flesh that clung to my bones, you could punch it
    in holes like clay;
The skin on my gums was a sullen black, and slowly
    peeling away.

I was sure enough in a direful fix, and often I wondered
    why
They did not take the chance that was left and leave me
    alone to die,
Or finish me off with a dose of dope—so utterly lost was I.

But no; they brewed me the green-spruce tea, and nursed
    me there like a child;
And the homicide he was good to me, and bathed my sores
    and smiled;
And the thief he starved that I might be fed, and his eyes
    were kind and mild.

Yet they were woefully wicked men, and often at night in
    pain
I heard the murderer speak of his deed and dream it over
    again;

I heard the poor thief sorrowing for the dead self he had
    slain.

I'll never forget that bitter dawn, so evil, askew and gray,
When they wrapped me round in the skins of beasts and
    they bore me to a sleigh,
And we started out with the nearest post a hundred miles
    away.

I'll never forget the trail they broke, with its tense,
    unuttered woe;
And the crunch, crunch, crunch as their snowshoes sank
    through the crust of the hollow snow;
And my breath would fail, and every beat of my heart was
    like a blow.

And oftentimes I would die the death, yet wake up to life
    anew;
The sun would be all ablaze on the waste, and the sky a
    blighting blue,
And the tears would rise in my snow-blind eyes and furrow
    my cheeks like dew.

And the camps we made when their strength outplayed
    and the day was pinched and wan;
And oh, the joy of that blessed halt, and how I did dread
    the dawn;
And how I hated the weary men who rose and dragged me
    on.

And oh, how I begged to rest, to rest—the snow was so
    sweet a shroud;
And oh, how I cried when they urged me on, cried and
    cursed them aloud;

138

Yet on they strained, all racked and pained, and sorely
  their backs were bowed.

And then it was all like a lurid dream, and I prayed for a
  swift release
From the ruthless ones who would not leave me to die
  alone in peace;
Till I wakened up and I found myself at the post of the
  Mounted Police.

And there was my friend the murderer, and there was my
  friend the thief,
With bracelets of steel around their wrists, and wicked
  beyond belief:
But when they come to God's judgment seat—may I be
  allowed the brief.

                                          Robert W. Service

Jim Jones

O, listen for a moment, lads, and hear me tell my tale—
How o'er the sea from England's shore I was compelled to
  sail.
The jury says, "He's guilty, sir," and says the judge, says
  he—
"For life, Jim Jones, I'm sending you across the stormy sea;
And take my tip before you ship to join the iron gang,
Don't be too gay at Botany Bay, or else you'll surely
  hang—
Or else you'll hang," he says, says he—"and after that,
  Jim Jones,
High up upon the gallow tree the crows will pick your
  bones—

You'll have no chance for mischief then; remember what I
   say,
They'll flog the poaching out of you, out there at Botany
   Bay."

The winds blew high upon the sea, and the pirates came
   along,
But the soldiers on our convict ship were full five hundred
   strong,
They opened fire and somehow drove that pirate ship
   away.
I'd have rather joined that pirate ship than come to Botany
   Bay:
For night and day the irons clang, and like poor galley
   slaves
We toil, and toil, and when we die must fill dishonored
   graves.
But by and by I'll break my chains: into the bush I'll go,
And join the brave bushrangers there—Jack Donohoo and
   Co.;
And some dark night when everything is silent in the town
I'll kill the tyrants, one and all, and shoot the floggers
   down:
I'll give the Law a little shock: remember what I say,
They'll yet regret they sent Jim Jones in chains to Botany
   Bay.

Anonymous

The Dead Swagman

His rusted billy left beside the tree;
Under a root, most carefully tucked away,
His steel-rimmed glasses folded in their case

140

Of mildewed purple velvet; there he lies
In the sunny afternoon and takes his ease,
Curled like a possum within the hollow trunk.

He came one winter evening when the tree
Hunched its broad back against the rain, and made
His camp, and slept, and did not wake again.
Now white ants make a home within his skull:
His old friend Fire has walked across the hill
And blackened the old tree and the old man
And buried him half in ashes, where he lay.

It might be called a lonely death. The tree
Had its own alien life beneath the sun,
Yet both belong to the Bush, and now are one:
The roots and bones lie close among the soil,
And he ascends in leaves towards the sky.

Nancy Cato

The Man from Snowy River

There was movement at the station, for the word had
    passed around
    That the colt from old Regret had got away,
And had joined the wild bush horses—he was worth a
    thousand pound,
    So all the cracks had gathered to the fray.
All the tried and noted riders from the stations near and
    far
    Had mustered at the homestead overnight,
For the bushmen love hard riding where the wild bush
    horses are,
    And the stock horse snuffs the battle with delight.

There was Harrison, who made his pile when Pardon won
    the cup,
    The old man with his hair as white as snow;
But few could ride beside him when his blood was fairly
    up—
    He would go wherever horse and man could go.
And Clancy of the Overflow came down to lend a hand,
    No better horseman ever held the reins;
For never horse could throw him while the saddle girths
    would stand—
    He learned to ride while droving on the plains.

And one was there, a stripling on a small and weedy beast,
    He was something like a racehorse undersized,
With a touch of Timor pony—three parts thoroughbred at
    least—
    And such as are by mountain horsemen prized.
He was hard and tough and wiry—just the sort that won't
    say die—
    There was courage in his quick impatient tread;
And he bore the badge of gameness in his bright and fiery
    eye,
    And the proud and lofty carriage of his head.

But still so slight and weedy, one would doubt his power to
    stay,
    And the old man said, "That horse will never do
For a long and tiring gallop—lad, you'd better stop away,
    Those hills are far too rough for such as you."
So he waited, sad and wistful—only Clancy stood his
    friend—
    "I think we ought to let him come," he said;
"I warrant he'll be with us when he's wanted at the end,
    For both his horse and he are mountain bred.

He hails from Snowy River, up by Kosciusko's side,
  Where the hills are twice as steep and twice as rough;
Where a horse's hoofs strike firelight from the flint stones
    every stride,
  The man that holds his own is good enough.
And the Snowy River riders on the mountains make their
    home,
  Where the river runs those giant hills between;
I have seen full many horsemen since I first commenced to
    roam,
  But nowhere yet such horsemen have I seen."

So he went; they found the horses by the big mimosa
    clump,
  They raced away towards the mountain's brow,
And the old man gave his orders, "Boys, go at them from
    the jump,
  No use to try for fancy riding now.
And, Clancy, you must wheel them, try and wheel them
    to the right.
  Ride boldly, lad, and never fear the spills,
For never yet was rider that could keep the mob in sight,
  If once they gain the shelter of those hills."

So Clancy rode to wheel them—he was racing on the wing
  Where the best and boldest riders take their place,
And he raced his stock horse past them, and he made the
    ranges ring
  With the stock whip, as he met them face to face.
Then they halted for a moment, while he swung the
    dreaded lash,
  But they saw their well-loved mountains full in view,
And they charged beneath the stock whip with a sharp
    and sudden dash,
  And off into the mountain scrub they flew.

Then fast the horsemen followed, where the gorges deep
    and black
    Resounded to the thunder of their tread,
And the stock whips woke the echoes, and they fiercely
    answered back
    From cliffs and crags that beetled overhead.
And upward, ever upward, the wild horses held their way,
    Where mountain ash and kurrajong grew wide;
And the old man muttered fiercely, "We may bid the mob
    good day,
    No man can hold them down the other side."

When they reached the mountain's summit, even Clancy
    took a pull—
    It well might make the boldest hold their breath;
The wild hop scrub grew thickly, and the hidden ground
    was full
    Of wombat holes, and any slip was death.
But the man from Snowy River let the pony have his head,
    And he swung his stock whip round and gave a cheer,
And he raced him down the mountain like a torrent down
    its bed,
    While the others stood and watched in very fear.

He sent the flint stones flying, but the pony kept his feet,
    He cleared the fallen timber in his stride,
And the man from Snowy River never shifted in his seat—
    It was grand to see that mountain horseman ride.
Through the stringy barks and saplings, on the rough and
    broken ground,
    Down the hillside at a racing pace he went;
And he never drew the bridle till he landed safe and sound
    At the bottom of that terrible descent.

He was right among the horses as they climbed the farther
      hill,
   And the watchers on the mountain, standing mute,
Saw him ply the stock whip fiercely; he was right among
      them still,
   As he raced across the clearing in pursuit.
Then they lost him for a moment, where two mountain
      gullies met
   In the ranges—but a final glimpse reveals
On a dim and distant hillside the wild horses racing yet,
   With the man from Snowy River at their heels.

And he ran them singlehanded till their sides were white
      with foam;
   He followed like a bloodhound on their track,
Till they halted, cowed and beaten; then he turned their
      heads for home,
   And alone and unassisted brought them back.
But his hardy mountain pony he could scarcely raise a trot,
   He was blood from hip to shoulder from the spur;
But his pluck was still undaunted, and his courage fiery
      hot,
   For never yet was mountain horse a cur.

And down by Kosciusko, where the pine-clad ridges raise
   Their torn and rugged battlements on high,
Where the air is clear as crystal and the white stars fairly
      blaze
   At midnight in the cold and frosty sky,
And where around the Overflow the reedbeds sweep and
      sway
   To the breezes, and the rolling plains are wide,
The man from Snowy River is a household word today,
   And the stockmen tell the story of his ride.

                          A. B. ("Banjo") Paterson

The Man from Ironbark

It was the man from Ironbark who struck the Sydney town,
He wandered over street and park, he wandered up and
    down,
He loitered here, he loitered there, till he was like to drop,
Until at last in sheer despair he sought a barber's shop.
" 'Ere! shave my beard and whiskers off, I'll be a man of
    mark,
I'll go and do the Sydney toff up home in Ironbark."

The barber man was small and flash, as barbers mostly are,
He wore a strike-your-fancy sash, he smoked a huge cigar:
He was a humorist of note and keen at repartee,
He laid the odds and kept a "tote," whatever that may be,
And when he saw our friend arrive, he whispered, "Here's
    a lark!
Just watch me catch him all alive, this man from Ironbark."

There were some gilded youths that sat along the barber's
    wall.
Their eyes were dull, their heads were flat, they had no
    brains at all;
To them the barber passed the wink, his dexter eyelid shut,
"I'll make this bloomin' yokel think his bloomin' throat is
    cut."
And as he soaped and rubbed it in he made a rude remark:
"I s'pose the flats is pretty green up there in Ironbark."

A grunt was all reply he got; he shaved the bushman's chin,
Then made the water boiling hot and dipped the razor in.
He raised his hand, his brow grew black, he paused awhile
    to gloat,

146

Then slashed the red-hot razor-back across his victim's
  throat;
Upon the newly shaven skin it made a livid mark—
No doubt it fairly took him in—the man from Ironbark.

He fetched a wild up-country yell might wake the dead to
  hear,
And though his throat, he knew full well, was cut from
  ear to ear,
He struggled gamely to his feet, and faced the murderous
  foe:
"You've done for me! You dog, I'm beat! One hit before I
  go!
I only wish I had a knife, you blessed murderous shark!
But you'll remember all your life the man from Ironbark."

He lifted up his hairy paw, with one tremendous clout
He landed on the barber's jaw, and knocked the barber out.
He set to work with tooth and nail, he made the place a
  wreck;
He grabbed the nearest gilded youth, and tried to break
  his neck.
And all the while his throat he held to save his vital spark,
And "Murder! Bloody murder!" yelled the man from
  Ironbark.

A peeler man who heard the din came in to see the show;
He tried to run the bushman in, but he refused to go.
And when at last the barber spoke, and said, " 'Twas all in
  fun—
'Twas just a little harmless joke, a trifle overdone."
"A joke!" he cried. "By George, that's fine; a lively sort of
  lark;
I'd like to catch that murdering swine some night in
  Ironbark."

And now while round the shearing floor the listening
    shearers gape,
He tells the story o'er and o'er, and brags of his escape.
"Them barber chaps what keeps a tote, by George, I've
    had enough,
One tried to cut my bloomin' throat, but thank the Lord
    it's tough."
And whether he's believed or not, there's one thing to
    remark,
That flowing beards are all the go way up in Ironbark.

A. B. ("Banjo") Paterson

The Swagless Swaggie

This happened many years ago
    Before the bush was cleared,
When every man was six foot high
    And wore a flowing beard.
One very hot and windy day,
    Along the old coach road,
Towards Joe Murphy's halfway house
    A bearded bushman strode.

He was a huge and heavy man,
    Well over six foot high,
An old slouch hat was on his head,
    And murder in his eye.
No billycan was in his hand,
    No heavy swag he bore,

148

But deep and awful were the oaths
   That swagless swaggie swore.

At last he reached the shanty door.
   Into the bar he burst.
He dumped his hat upon the floor,
   And cursed and cursed and cursed.
A neighboring shed had just cut out;
   The bar was nearly full
Of shearers and of bullockies
   Who'd come to cart the wool.

They were a rough and ready lot,
   The bushmen gathered there,
But every man was stricken dumb,
   To hear the stranger swear.
He cursed the bush, he cursed mankind,
   The whole wide universe.
It froze their very blood to hear
   That swagless swaggie curse.

Joe Murphy seized an empty pot
   And filled it brimming full.
The stranger raised it to his lips
   And took a mighty pull.
This seemed to cool him down a bit;
   He finished off the ale,
And to the crowd around the bar
   He told his awful tale.

"I met the Ben Hall gang," he said,
   "The blankards stuck me up!
They pinched me billy, pinched me swag,
   They pinched me flamin' pup!
They turned me pockets inside out,

And took me only quid!
I never thought they'd pinch me pipe—
  But swelp me gawd they did!

"I spoke to 'em as man to man,
  I said I'd fight 'em all;
I would have broke O'Meally's neck,
  And tanned the hide of Hall.
They only laughed, and said good-by,
  And rode away to brag
Of how they stuck a swaggie up
  And robbed him of his swag.

"I never done 'em any harm,
  I thought 'em decent chaps.
But now I wouldn't raise a hand
  To save 'em from the traps.
I'm finished with the bush for good,
  I'm off to Wagga town
Where they won't stick a swaggie up
  Or take a swaggie down."

The bushmen were a decent lot,
  As bushmen mostly are.
They filled the stranger up with beer;
  The hat went round the bar.
The shearers threw some blankets in
  To make another swag,
The rousers gave a billycan
  And brand new tucker bag;

Joe Murphy gave a meerschaum pipe
  He hadn't smoked for years.
The stranger was too full of words,

His eyes were dim with tears.
The ringer shouted drinks all round
   And then, to top it up,
The babbling brook, the shearers' cook,
   Gave him a kelpie pup.

Next day, an hour before the dawn,
   The stranger took the track
Complete with pup and billycan,
   His swag upon his back.
Along the most forsaken roads,
   Intent on dodging graft,
He headed for the Great North West,
   And laughed, and laughed, and laughed.

Edward Harrington

Down and Out

So, you've come to the tropics, heard all you had to do
Was sit in the shade of a coconut glade while the dollars
   roll in to you.
They told you that at the bureau? Did you get the statistics
   all straight?
Well, hear what it did to another kid, before you decide
   your fate.
You don't go down with a hard, short fall—you just sort of
   shuffle along
And loosen your load of the moral code, till you can't tell
   the right from the wrong.

I started out to be honest, with everything on the square,
But a man can't fool with the Golden Rule in a crowd that
   won't play fair.

'Twas a case of riding a dirty race, or of being an also-ran;
My only hope was to steal and dope the horse of another
man.

I pulled a deal at Guayaquil in an Inca silver mine,
But before they found it was salted ground I was safe in
Argentine.
I made short weight on the River Plate, when running a
freighter there;
And I cracked a crib on a rich estate without even turning
a hair.

But the deal that will everlastingly bar my soul
When it knocks at Heaven's doors,
Was peddling booze to the Santa Cruz, and Winchester
forty-fours.
Made unafraid by my kindly aid, the drunk-crazed brutes
came down
And left in a shivering, blazing mass a flourishing border
town.

I was next in charge of a smuggler's barge off the coast of
Yucatan,
But she sank to hell off Cozonel one night in a hurricane.
I got to shore on a broken oar, in the filthy, shrieking dark;
With the other two of the good ship's crew converted into
shark.

From a limestone cliff I flagged a skiff with a pair of salt-
soaked jeans,
And I worked my way, for I couldn't pay, on a fruiter to
New Orleans.
It's kind of a habit, the tropics; it gets you worse than rum;
You'll get away and swear you'll stay, but it calls, and back
you come.

Six years went by before I was back on the job,
Running a war in Salvador, with an ugly, barefoot mob;
I was General Santiago Hicks at the head of a grand revolt,
And my only friend from start to end was a punishing
    army Colt.
I might have been a president, a prosperous man of means,
But a gunboat came and blocked my game with a hundred
    and ten marines.

So I awoke from my dream, dead broke—drifted from bad
    to worse:
Sank as low as a man can go who walks with an empty
    purse.
But stars, they say, appear by day, when you're down in a
    deep, black pit;
My lucky star found me that way, when I was about to
    quit.

On a fiery hot, flea-ridden cot, I was down with the yellow
    jack,
Alone in the bush and all but dead, when she found me and
    nursed me back.
She came like the miracle man of old and opened my poor
    blind eyes,
And upon me shone a bright new dawn as I turned my face
    to the skies.

There was pride and grace in her brown young face,
For hers was the blood of kings;
In her eyes shone the glory of empires gone,
And the secret of world-old things.

We were spliced in a Yankee meeting house on the land
    of your Uncle Sam,

And I drew my pay from the U.S.A., for I worked at the
    Gatun Dam.
Then the Devil sent his right-hand man (I might have
    expected he would)
And he took her life with a long, thin knife, because she
    was straight and good.

Within me died hope, honor, pride—all but a primitive will
To hunt him down on his blood-red trail—find him and
    kill, and kill.
Through logwood swamps and chicle camps I hunted him
    many a moon,
And I found my man in a long pit-pen, by the side of a
    blue lagoon.

The chase was o'er at the farthest shore—it ended my two
    years' quest;
And I left him there with a vacant stare and a John Crow
    on his chest.
You see these punctures on my arm? Do you want to know
    what they mean?
Those marks were left by fingers deft of my trained nurse,
    "Miss Morphine."

Of course you'll say that's worse than drink; it's possible,
    too, you're right;
At least it drives away the things that come and peer in
    the night.
There is a homestead down in an old Maine town, with
    lilacs around the gate,
And the Northerners whisper, "It might have been," but
    the truth has come too late.

They say they'll give me one month to live—a month or a
    year is the same;

154

I haven't the heart to play my part to the end of a losing
   game.
For whenever you play, whatever the way, for stakes that
   are large or small,
The claws of the tropics will gather your pile and the dealer
   gets it all.

Clarence Leonard Hay

ROBBERS AND OUTLAWS

The Lament
of the Border Cattle Thief

O woe is me for the merry life
   I led beyond the Bar,
And a treble woe for my winsome wife
   That weeps at Shalimar.

They have taken away my long jezail,[1]
   My shield and saber fine,
And heaved me into the Central Jail
   For lifting of the kine.

The steer may low within the byre,
   The Jat [2] may tend his grain,
But there'll be neither loot nor fire
   Till I come back again.

And God have mercy on the Jat
   When once my fetters fall,
And Heaven defend the farmer's hut
   When I am loosed from thrall.

[1] *jezail*: native gun
[2] *Jat*: an Indo-Aryan of the Punjab

It's woe to bend the stubborn back
　　Above the grinching quern,[3]
It's woe to hear the leg-bar clack
　　And jingle when I turn!

But for the sorrow and the shame,
　　The brand on me and mine,
I'll pay you back in leaping flame
　　And loss of the butchered kine.

For every cow I spared before—
　　In charity set free—
If I may reach my hold once more
　　I'll reive an honest three.

For every time I raised the lowe
　　That scared the dusty plain,
By sword and cord, by torch and tow
　　I'll light the land with twain!

Ride hard, ride hard to Abazai,
　　Young Sahib with the yellow hair—
Lie close, lie close as Khuttucks[4] lie,
　　Fat herds below Bonair!

The one I'll shoot at twilight-tide,
　　At dawn I'll drive the other;
The black shall mourn for hoof and hide,
　　The white man for his brother.

---

[3] *grinching quern*: a crude hand grinder
[4] *Khuttucks*: A tribe on the Indian frontier

'Tis war, red war, I'll give you then,
   War till my sinews fail;
For the wrong you have done to a chief of men,
   And a thief of the Zukka Kheyl.

And if I fall to your hand afresh
   I give you leave for the sin,
That you cram my throat with the foul pig's flesh,
   And swing me in the skin!

Rudyard Kipling

The Outlaw

Oh, I wadna be a yeoman, mither, to follow my father's
   trade,
To bow my back in miry banks, at pleugh and hoe and
   spade.
Stinting wife, and bairns, and kye, to fat some courtier
   lord,—
Let them die o' rent wha like, mither, and I'll die by sword.

Nor I wadna be a clerk, mither, to bide aye ben,[1]
Scrabbling ower the sheets o' parchment with a weary
   weary pen;
Looking through the lang stane windows at a narrow strip
   o' sky,
Like a laverock[2] in a withy cage, until I pine away and die.

Nor I wadna be a merchant, mither, in his lang furred
   gown,
Trailing strings o' footsore horses through the noisy dusty
   town;

[1] *ben*: within, indoors
[2] *laverock*: lark

Louting low to knights and ladies, fumbling o'er his wares,
Telling lies, and scraping siller, heaping cares on cares.

Nor I wadna be a soldier, mither, to dice wi' ruffian bands,
Pining weary months in castles, looking over wasted lands.
Smoking byres, and shrieking women, and the grewsome
    sights o' war—
There's blood on my hand eneugh, mither; it's ill to make
    it mair.

If I had married a wife, mither, I might ha' been douce and
    still,
And sat at hame by the ingle side to crack [3] and laugh my
    fill;
Sat at hame wi' the woman I looed, and wi' bairnies at my
    knee:
But death is bauld, and age is cauld, and luve's no for me.

For when first I stirred in your side, mither, ye ken full well
How you lay all night up among the deer out on the open
    fell;
And so it was that I won the heart to wander far and near,
Caring neither for land nor lassie, but the bonnie dun deer.

Yet I am not a losel [4] and idle, mither, nor a thief that
    steals;
I do but hunt God's cattle, upon God's ain hills;
For no man buys and sells the deer, and the bonnie fells are
    free
To a belted knight with hawk on hand, and a gangrel
    loon like me.

[3] *crack*: chat, gossip, talk
[4] *losel*: ne'er-do-well, worthless person

So I'm aff and away to the muirs, mither, to hunt the deer,
Ranging far frae frowning faces, and the douce folk here;
Crawling up through burn and bracken, louping down the
    screes,
Looking out frae craig and headland, drinking up the
    simmer breeze.

Oh, the wafts o' heather honey, and the music o' the brae,
As I watch the great harts feeding, nearer, nearer a' the
    day.
Oh, to hark the eagle screaming, sweeping, ringing round
    the sky—
That's a bonnier life than stumbling ower the muck to colt
    and kye.

And when I'm ta'en and hangit, mither, a brittling[5] o' my
    deer,
Ye'll no leave your bairn to the corbie craws, to dangle in
    the air;
But ye'll send up my two douce brethren, and ye'll steal me
    frae the tree,
And bury me up on the brown brown muirs, where I aye
    looed to be.

Ye'll bury me 'twixt the brae and the burn, in a glen far
    away,
Where I may hear the heathcock craw, and the great harts
    bray;
And gin my ghaist can walk, mither, I'll go glowering at
    the sky,
The livelong night on the black hillsides where the dun
    deer lie.

Charles Kingsley

[5] *brittling:* cutting up

Inscription from a Convict's Cell

For seven long years I have served them,
   And seven long years I have to stay,
For meeting a bloke in our alley
   And taking his ticker away.

                    Anonymous (nineteenth century)

Billy the Kid

Billy was a bad man
And carried a big gun,
He was always chasing women
And kept 'em on the run.

He shot men every morning
Just to make a morning meal—
If his gun ran out of bullets
He killed them with cold steel.

He kept folks in hot water,
And he stole from many a stage,
When his gut was full of liquor
He was always in a rage.

But one day he met a man
Who was a whole lot badder—
And now he's dead—
And we ain't none the sadder.

                    American ballad

Brennan on the Moor

It's of a fearless highwayman a story I will tell.
His name was Willie Brennan, in Ireland he did dwell;
And on the Kilworth mountains he commenced his wild
   career,
Where many a wealthy gentleman before him shook with
   fear.

A brace of loaded pistols he carried night and day;
He never robbed a poor man upon the King's highway;
But what he'd taken from the rich, like Turpin and Black
   Bess,
He always did divide it with the widows in distress.

One night he robbed a man of the name of Pedlar Bawn;
They traveling on together till the day began to dawn,
The pedlar seeing his money gone, likewise his watch and
   chain,
He at once encountered Brennan and robbed him back
   again.

When Brennan saw the pedlar was as good a man as he,
He took him on the highway, his companion for to be;
The pedlar threw away his pack without any more delay,
And proved a faithful comrade until his dying day.

One day upon the highway, as Willie he sat down,
He met the Mayor of Cashel a mile outside the town;
The Mayor he knew his features; "I think, young man,"
   says he,
"Your name is Willie Brennan, you must come along with
   me."

As Brennan's wife had gone to town, provisions for to buy,
When she saw her Willie, she began to weep and cry;
He says, "Give me that tenpenny"; as soon as Willie spoke,
She handed him a blunderbuss from underneath her cloak.

Then with this loaded blunderbuss, the truth I will unfold,
He made the Mayor to tremble, and robbed him of his
    gold;
One hundred pound was offered for his apprehension
    there,
And he with his horse and saddle to the mountains did
    repair.

Then Brennan being a outlaw, upon the mountains high,
Where cavalry and infantry to take him they did try;
He laughed at them with scorn, until at length it's said,
By a false-hearted young man he was basely betrayed.

In the County Tipperary, in a place they call Clonmore,
Willie Brennan and his comrade that day did suffer sore;
He lay amongst the fern, which was thick upon the field,
And nine wounds he did receive, before that he did yield.

Then Brennan and his companion, knowing they were
    betrayed,
He with the mounted cavalry a noble battle made;
He lost his foremost finger which was shot off by a ball,
So Brennan and his comrade, they were taken after all.

So they were taken prisoners; in irons they were bound,
And conveyed to Clonmel jail where strong walls did them
    surround;
They were tried and found guilty; the judge made this
    reply:

166

"For robbing on the King's highway, you're both
   condemned to die."

Farewell unto my wife, and to my children three,
Likewise my aged father; he may shed tears for me;
And to my loving mother, who tore her gray locks and
   cried,
Saying, "I wish, Willie Brennan, in your cradle you had
   died."

                    Irish ballad

Robin Hood and Little John

When Robin Hood was twenty years old,
   He happened to meet Little John,
A jolly, brisk blade, right fit for the trade,
   For he was a lusty young man.

Though he was called Little, his limbs they were large,
   And his length it was seven foot high;
Whenever he came, they quaked at his name,
   For soon he would make them all fly.

How they came acquainted, I'll tell you in brief,
   If you will but listen awhile.
For this very jest, among all the rest,
   I think it may cause you to smile.

They happened to meet on a long narrow bridge,
   And neither of them would give way.
Then spoke Robin Hood as he sturdily stood,
   "I'll show you right Nottingham play.

"The name of a coward," said Robin, "I scorn,
    Wherefore my long bow I'll lay by;
And now, for thy sake, a staff will I take,
    The strength of thy manhood to try."

Then Robin Hood stepped to a thicket of trees,
    And broke off a bough of ground oak;
Now this being done, away did he run
    To the stranger, and merrily spoke:

"My staff it is trusty and lusty and tough,
    Now here on the bridge we will play;
Whoever falls in, the other shall win
    The battle, and so we'll away."

"With all of my heart," the stranger replied;
    "I scorn in the least to give out."
This said, they fell to it without more dispute,
    And their staffs they did flourish about.

And first Robin Hood gave the stranger a bang,
    So hard that it made his bones ring;
The stranger he said, "This must be repaid,
    I'll give you as good as you bring.

"So long as I'm able to handle a staff,
    To die in your debt, friend, I scorn."
Then to it each goes, and followed their blows,
    As if they'd been threshing the corn.

The stranger gave Robin a crack on the crown,
    Which caused the red blood to appear;
Then Robin, enraged, more fiercely engaged,
    And followed with blows more severe.

168

O then into fury the stranger he grew,
    And gave him a furious look,
And with it a blow that laid him full low,
    And tumbled him into the brook.

"I prithee, good fellow, O where art thou now?"
    The stranger, in laughter, he cried.
Quoth bold Robin Hood, "Good faith, in the flood,
    And floating along with the tide.

"I needs must acknowledge thou art a brave soul,
    With thee I'll no longer contend;
For needs must I say, thou hast won the day;
    Our battle shall be at an end."

Then unto the bank he did presently wade,
    And pulled himself out by a thorn;
While done, at the last he blew a loud blast
    Straightway on his fine bugle horn.

The echo of this through the valleys did fly,
    At which his stout bowmen appeared,
All clothed in green, most gay to be seen;
    So up to their master they steered.

"O, what is the matter?" quoth William Stutly;
    "Good master, you're wet to the skin."
"No matter," quoth he, "the lad which you see
    In fighting hath tumbled me in."

"He shall not go scot free," the other replied;
    So straight they were seizing him there,
To duck him likewise; but Robin Hood cries,
    "This man's a stout fellow. Forbear!

"There's no one shall wrong thee, friend. Be not afraid;
    These bowmen upon me do wait;
There's threescore and nine. If thou wilt be mine,
    Thou shalt wear my own livery straight."

"O here is my hand," the stranger replied,
    "I'll serve thee with all of my heart;
My name is John Little, a man of good mettle;
    Ne'er doubt me, for I'll play my part."

"His name shall be altered," quoth William Stutly,
    "And I will his godfather be;
Prepare then a feast, and none of the least,
    For we will be merry," quoth he.

When all his bowmen, which stood in a ring,
    And were of the Nottingham breed,
Brave Stutly came then, with seven yeomen,
    And did in this manner proceed:

"This infant was called John Little," quoth he,
    "Which name shall be changed anon;
The words we'll transpose, so wherever he goes,
    His name shall be called Little John."

Then Robin he took the handsome young man,
    And clothed him from top to his toe
In garments of green, most gay to be seen,
    And gave him a mighty longbow.

Then music and dancing did finish the day;
    At length, when the sunlight sank low,
Then with all of their goods they left the green woods,
    And unto their caves they did go.

And so, ever after, as long as he lived,
 Although he was tall evermore,
Yet, nevertheless, the truth to express
 Little John was the name that he bore.

English folk ballad

The Wild Colonial Boy

There was a wild colonial boy, Jack Donahoe by name,
Of poor but honest parents he was born in Castlemain.
He was his father's dearest hope, his mother's pride and
 joy.
O, fondly did his parents love their Wild Colonial Boy.

Chorus:

*So ride with me, my hearties, we'll cross the mountains
 high.*
Together we will plunder, together we will die.
*We'll wander through the valleys and gallop o'er the
 plains,*
*For we scorn to live in slavery, bound down with iron
 chains!*

He was scarcely sixteen years of age when he left his
 father's home,
A convict to Australia, across the seas to roam.
They put him in the Iron Gang in the Government employ,
But ne'er an iron on earth could hold the Wild Colonial
 Boy.

And when they sentenced him to hang to end his wild
 career,
With a loud shout of defiance bold Donahoe broke clear.

He robbed those wealthy squatters, their stock he did
   destroy,
But never a trap in the land could catch the Wild Colonial
   Boy.

Then one day when he was cruising near the broad
   Nepean's side,
From out the thick Bringelly bush the horse police did ride.
"Die or resign, Jack Donahoe!" they shouted in their joy.
"I'll fight this night with all my might!" cried the Wild
   Colonial Boy.

He fought six rounds with the horse police before the fatal
   ball,
Which pierced his heart with cruel smart, caused Donahoe
   to fall.
And then he closed his mournful eyes, his pistol an empty
   toy,
Crying: "Parents dear, O say a prayer for the Wild
   Colonial Boy."

Australian folk ballad

Charley Lee

A low moon shone on the desert land and the sage was
   silver white,
As Lee—a thong round hand and hand—stood straight in
   the lantern light.
  "You have strung up Red and Burke," said he,
  "And you say that the next will be Charley Lee,
  But there's never a rope was made for me."
And he laughed in the quiet night.

172

They shaped the noose and they flicked the rope and over
    the limb it fell,
And Charley Lee saw the ghost of hope go glimmering
    down to hell.
    Two shadows swung from the cottonwood tree,
    And the wind went whispering, "Charley Lee,"
    For the turning shadows would soon be three,
And never a stone to tell.

"Have ye more to say for yourself?" said Gray, "a message
    the like, or prayer?
If ye have, then hasten and have your say. We trailed and
    we trapped ye fair,
    With fire and iron at Hidden Sink,
    Where none but the stolen horses drink.
    And the chain but wanted a final link.
Ye were riding my red roan mare."

"But prove your property first," said Lee. "Would you call
    the mare your own,
With never a brand or mark to see, or name to the big red
    roan?
    But strip the saddle and turn her loose,
    And I'll show that the mare is my own cayuse.
    And I don't—then take it a fair excuse,
To tighten the rope you've thrown."

Gaunt, grim faces and steady eyes were touched with a
    somber look,
And hands slipped slowly to belted thighs and held on a
    finger-crook,
    For Gray of Mesa who claimed the mare,
    Had talked too much as he led them there,
    Nor other among them knew the lair,
So a grip on their haste they took.

"Give him a chance," said Monty Wade, and, "What is the
  use?" said Blake.
"He's done," said Harney; "his string is played. But we'll
  give him an even break."
  So they led the mare to the cottonwood tree,
  Nor saddle nor bridle nor rope had she.
  "Bonnie, come here!" said Charley Lee,
And soft was the word he spake.

The roan mare came and she nosed his side and nuzzled
  him friendly-wise;
"Kneel!" cried Lee, and he leaped astride and fled as the
  swallow flies.
  Flashes followed his flight in vain,
  Bullets spattered the ground like rain,
  Hoofs drummed far on the midnight plain,
And a low moon rode the skies.

Dawn broke red on the desert land where the turning
  shadows fell,
And the wind drove over the rolling sand with a
  whimpering ebb and swell,
  Whimpering, whispering, "Charley Lee,"
  As south on the red roan mare rode he,
  Yet the turning shadows they were three,
And never a stone to tell.

Henry Herbert Knibbs

Clever Tom Clinch

Going to be Hanged, 1727

As clever Tom Clinch, while the rabble was bawling,
Rode stately through Holborn to die in his calling,
He stopped at the George for a bottle of sack,
And promised to pay for it when he came back.
His waistcoat, and stockings, and breeches, were white;
His cap had a new cherry ribbon to tie't.
The maids to the doors and the balconies ran,
And said, "Lack-a-day, he's a proper young man!"
But, as from the windows the ladies he spied,
Like a beau in the box, he bowed low on each side!
And when his last speech the loud hawkers did cry,
He swore from his cart it was all a damned lie!
The hangman for pardon fell down on his knee;
Tom gave him a kick in the guts for his fee:
Then said, "I must speak to the people a little;
But I'll see you all damned before I will whittle.
My honest friend Wild (may he long hold his place)
He lengthen'd my life with a whole year of grace.
Take courage, dear comrades, and be not afraid,
Nor slip this occasion to follow your trade;
My conscience is clear, and my spirits are calm,
And thus I go off, without prayer-book or psalm;
Then follow the practice of clever Tom Clinch,
Who hung like a hero, and never would flinch."

Jonathan Swift

BRAWLERS

A Great Fight

There was a man in Arkansaw
   As let his passions rise,
And not unfrequently picked out
   Some other varmint's eyes.

His name was Tuscaloosa Sam
   And often he would say,
"There's not a cuss in Arkansaw
   I can't whip any day."

One morn, a stranger passin' by
   Heard Sammy talkin' so,
And down he scrambled from his hoss,
   And off his coat did go.

He sorter kinder shut one eye,
   And spit into his hand,
And put his ugly head one side,
   And twitched his trousers' band.

"My boy," says he, "it's my belief,
  Whomever you may be,
That I kin make you screech, and smell
  Pertiklor agony."

"I'm thar," said Tuscaloosa Sam,
  And chucked his hat away;
"I'm thar," says he, and buttoned up
  As far as buttons may.

He thundered on the stranger's mug,
  The stranger pounded he;
And oh! the way them critters fit
  Was beautiful to see.

They clinched like two rampageous bears,
  And then went down a bit;
They swore a stream of six-inch oaths
  And fit, and fit, and fit.

When Sam would try to work away,
  And on his pegs to git,
The stranger'd pull him back; and so,
  They fit, and fit, and fit!

Then like a pair of lobsters, both
  Upon the ground were knit,
And yet the varmints used their teeth,
  And fit, and fit, and fit! !

The sun of noon was high above,
  And hot enough to split,
But only riled the fellers more,
  That fit, and fit, and fit! ! !

180

The stranger snapped at Sammy's nose,
    And shortened it a bit;
And then they both swore awful hard,
    And fit, and fit, and fit! ! ! !

The mud it flew, the sky grew dark,
    And all the litenins lit;
But still them critters rolled about,
    And fit, and fit, and fit! ! ! ! !

First Sam on top, then t'other chap;
    When one would make a hit,
The other'd smell the grass; and so
    They fit, and fit, and fit! ! ! ! ! !

The night came on, the stars shone out
    As bright as wimmen's wit;
And still them fellers swore and gouged,
    And fit, and fit, and fit! ! ! ! ! ! !

The neighbors heard the noise they made,
    And thought an earthquake lit;
Yet all the while 'twas him and Sam
    As fit, and fit, and fit! ! ! ! ! ! ! !

For miles around the noise was heard;
    Folks couldn't sleep a bit,
Because them two rantankerous chaps
    Still fit, and fit, and fit! ! ! ! ! ! ! ! !

But jist at cock-crow, suddenly,
    There came an awful pause,
And I and my old man run out
    To ascertain the cause.

The sun was rising in the yeast,
　And lit the whole concern;
But not a sign of either chap
　Was found at any turn.

Yet, in the region where they fit,
　We found, to our surprise,
One pint of buttons, two big knives,
　Some whiskers, and four eyes!

Robert Henry Newell

Simon Legree—A Negro Sermon

Legree's big house was white and green.
His cotton fields were the best to be seen.
He had strong horses and opulent cattle,
And bloodhounds bold, with chains that would rattle.
His garret was full of curious things:
Books of magic, bags of gold,
And rabbits' feet on long twine strings.
But he went down to the Devil.

Legree he sported a brass-buttoned coat,
A snakeskin necktie, a blood-red shirt.
Legree he had a beard like a goat,
And a thick hairy neck, and eyes like dirt.
His puffed-out cheeks were fish-belly white,
He had great long teeth, and an appetite.
He ate raw meat, 'most every meal,
And rolled his eyes till the cat would squeal.

His fist was an enormous size
To mash poor niggers that told him lies:

182

He was surely a witch-man in disguise.
But he went down to the Devil.

He wore hip boots, and would wade all day
To capture his slaves that had fled away.
But he went down to the Devil.

He beat poor Uncle Tom to death
Who prayed for Legree with his last breath.
Then Uncle Tom to Eva flew,
To the high sanctoriums bright and new;
And Simon Legree stared up beneath,
And cracked his heels, and ground his teeth:
And went down to the Devil.

He crossed the yard in the storm and gloom;
He went into his grand front room.
He said, "I killed him, and I don't care."
He kicked a hound, he gave a swear;
He tightened his belt, he took a lamp,
Went down cellar to the webs and damp.
There in the middle of the moldy floor
He heaved up a slab; he found a door—
And went down to the Devil.

His lamp blew out, but his eyes burned bright.
Simon Legree stepped down all night—
Down, down to the Devil.
Simon Legree he reached the place,
He saw one half of the human race,
He saw the Devil on a wide green throne,
Gnawing the meat from a big ham bone,
And he said to Mister Devil:
    "I see that you have much to eat—

A red ham bone is surely sweet.
I see that you have lion's feet;
I see your frame is fat and fine,
I see you drink your poison wine—
Blood and burning turpentine."

And the Devil said to Simon Legree:
    "I like your style, so wicked and free.
    Come sit and share my throne with me,
    And let us bark and revel."
And there they sit and gnash their teeth,
And each one wears a hopvine wreath.
They are matching pennies and shooting craps,
They are playing poker and taking naps.
And old Legree is fat and fine:
He eats the fire, he drinks the wine—
Blood and burning turpentine—
    Down, down with the Devil;
        Down, down with the Devil;
            Down, down with the Devil.

Vachel Lindsay

Boxer

Poised, relaxed, as a cat that waits,
   Too obviously bored, for the mouse to venture,
You endure the familiar ritual. They lace
   The gloves on, lead you to the center,
The half-heard mutter and the touching hands.
   The lights insist upon your thinning hair,

The best years are behind. Nothing at stake
   Tonight; purse and crowd are small;
Only another fight among the hundred-odd
   Since boyhood and the animal
Tumblings in the street. Never a champion:
   You fought him once, but lost the call;

And not again. These are the final years
   As the aging body threatens to rebel
And they send the upstart boys to take you.
   One will. But not tonight. The bell
Calls you to work, and to your finest night.
   The crowd held silent by your fluent spell,

For once not screaming for the knockout punch
   You never had, watches an adept in an art
That, like an actor's, lives in the splendid moment
   And the betraying memory. You dart
The left hand like a bird that, roused to danger,
   Rakes at the hunter's eyes, and start

The young blood flowing as the right hand pounds
   The ribs and belly and you move away,

Then in, tense and pure and timeless
    In your perfect dance. Coolly you display
The repertoire of moves and punches mastered
    Through the dull years of sweat for pay.

You win. Time, masked as this beaten boy,
    Has his hand shaken and his matted hair
Ruffled by your glove. You shower, dress,
    Quietly collect your winner's share,
And leave, a tired workman going home,
    Who carved a marble image on the air.

                                    Joseph P. Clancy

Mastering the Craft

To make the big time you must learn
The basic moves: left jab and hook,
The fast one-two, right cross; the block
And counterpunch; the way to turn
Opponents on the ropes; the feint
To head or body; uppercut;
To move inside the swing and set
Your man up for the kill. But don't
Think that this is all; a mere
Beginning only. It is through
Fighting often you will grow
Accomplished in maneuvers more
Subtle than the textbooks know:
How to change your style to meet
The unexpected move that might
Leave you open to the blow
That puts the lights out for the night.
The same with poets: they must train,

Practice meter's footwork, learn
The old iambic left and right,
To change the pace and how to hold
The big punch till the proper time,
Jab away with accurate rhyme;
Adapt the style or be knocked cold.
But first the groundwork must be done;
Those poets who have never learned
The first moves of the game, they can't
Hope to win.
                    Yet here comes one,
No style at all, untrained and fat,
Who still contrives to knock you flat.

Vernon Scannell

Street Gang

Everywhere they are waiting. In silence.
In boredom. Staring into space.
Reflecting on nothing, or on violence
That is long since past. Wondering.
Wondering what will happen next.
Whatever it is is beyond their control
Or understanding. They are waiting. Not vexed
By any thoughts of the uncertain future
(Apparently); absorbed in the present
Shot through with spasms of the violent
Past. They are waiting. . . .
                              Coffee cups
Battle. Matches flare. Cigarettes
Glow in the darkness of the milk bar
Or the drugstore. Hour after hour
They sit, indistinguishable

In the darkness: oblivious of who they are
Or what they want: except to be together.

Then suddenly it happens. A motorcycle
Explodes outside, a cup smashes,
They are on their feet, identified
At last as living creatures.
The universal silence is shattered,
The law overthrown, chaos
Has come again. . . .
                    The victim has been kicked,
Gouged, stamped on, crucified.
His blood streams across the pavement.
And none of them knows why.
Tomorrow their endless vigil
Will begin again. Perhaps nothing will happen.
Or perhaps, this time, a single
Scapegoat will not suffice. . . .

H. Webster

First Fight

Tonight, then, is the night;
Stretched on the massage table,
Wrapped in his robe, he breathes
Liniment and sweat
And tries to close his ears
To the roaring of the crowd,
A murky sea of noise
That bears upon its tide
The frail sound of the bell
And brings the cunning fear
That he might not do well,

188

Not fear of bodily pain
But that his tight-lipped pride
Might be sent crashing down,
His white ambition slain,
Knocked spinning the glittering crown.
How could his spirit bear
That ignominious fall?
Not hero but a clown
Spurned or scorned by all.
The thought appalls, and he
Feels sudden envy for
The roaring crowd outside
And wishes he were there
Anonymous and safe,
Calm in the tolerant air,
Would almost choose to be
Anywhere but here.

II

The door blares open suddenly,
The room is sluiced with row;
His second says, "We're on next fight,
We'd better get going now.
You got your gumshield, haven't you?
Just loosen up—that's right—
Don't worry, Boy, you'll be O.K.
Once you start to fight."

Out of the dressing room, along
The neutral passage to
The yelling cavern where the ring
Through the haze of blue
Tobacco smoke is whitewashed by
The aching glare of light:

Geometric ropes are stretched as taut
As this boy's nerves are tight.

And now he's in his corner where
He tries to look at ease;
He feels the crowd's sharp eyes as they
Prick and pry and tease;
He hears them murmur like the sea
Or some great dynamo:
They are not hostile yet they wish
To see his lifeblood flow.
His adversary enters now;
The boy risks one quick glance;
He does not see any enemy
But something there by chance.
Not human even, but a cold
Abstraction to defeat,
A problem to be solved by guile,
Quick hands, and knowing feet.
The fighters' names are shouted out;
They leave their corners for
The touch of gloves and brief commands;
The disciplines of war.
Back in their corners, stripped of robes,
They hear the bell clang ONE
Brazen syllable which says
The battle has begun.

III

Bite on gumshield
Guard held high,
The crowd are silenced
All sounds die.
Lead with the left,

Again, again;
Watch for the opening,
Feint and then
Hook to the body
But he's blocked it and
Slammed you back
With a fierce right hand.
Hang on grimly
The fog will clear,
Sweat in your nostrils
Grease and fear.
You're hurt and staggering,
Shocked to know
That the story's altered:
He's the hero!

But the mist is clearing,
The referee snaps
A rapid warning
And he smartly taps
Your hugging elbow
And then you step back
Ready to counter
The next attack,
But the first round finishes
Without mishap.
You suck in the air
From the towel's skilled flap.
A voice speaks urgently
Close to your ear:
"Keep your left going, Boy,
Stop him getting near."
He wants to get close to you,
So jab him off hard;

When he tries to slip below,
Never mind your guard,
Crack him with a solid right
Hit him on the chin,
A couple downstairs
And then he'll pack it in!

Slip in the gumshield
Bite on it hard.
Keep him off with your left,
Never drop your guard.
Try a left hook,
But he crosses with a right
Smack on your jaw
And Guy Fawkes night
Flashes and dazzles
Inside your skull,
Your knees go bandy
And you almost fall.
Keep the left jabbing,
Move around the ring,
Don't let him catch you with
Another hook or swing.
Keep your left working,
Keep it up high,
Stab it out straight and hard,
Again—above the eye.
Sweat in the nostrils,
But nothing now of fear,
You're moving smooth and confident
In comfortable gear.
Jab with the left again,
Quickly move away;
Feint and stab another in,
See him duck and sway.

NOW for the pay-off punch,
Smash it hard inside;
It thuds against his jaw, he falls,
Limbs spread wide.
And suddenly you hear the roar
Hoarse music of the crowd,
Voicing your hot ecstasy
Triumphant, male, and proud.

IV

Now, in the sleepless darkness of his room
The Boy, in bed, remembers. Suddenly
The victory tastes sour. The man he fought
Was not a thing, as lifeless as a broom
He was a man who hoped and trembled too;
What of him now? What was *he* going through?
And then the Boy bites hard on resolution:
Fighters can't pack pity with their gear,
And yet a bitter taste stays with the notion;
He's forced to swallow down one treacherous tear.
But that's the last. He is a boy no longer;
He is a man, a fighter, such as jeer
At those who make salt beads with melting eyes,
Whatever might cry out, is hurt, or dies.

Vernon Scannell

Abdullah Bulbul Amir

The sons of the Prophet are valiant and bold,
　　And quite unaccustomed to fear;
And the bravest of all was a man, so I'm told,
　　Called Abdullah Bulbul Amir.

When they wanted a man to encourage the van,
  Or harass the foe from the rear,
Storm fort or redoubt, they were sure to call out
  For Abdullah Bulbul Amir.

There are heroes in plenty, and well known to fame,
  In the legions that fight for the Czar;
But none of such fame as the man by the name
  Of Ivan Petrofsky Skovar.

He could imitate Irving, tell fortunes by cards,
  And play on the Spanish guitar;
In fact, quite the cream of the Muscovite guards
  Was Ivan Petrofsky Skovar.

One day this bold Muscovite shouldered his gun,
  Put on his most cynical sneer,
And was walking downtown when he happened to run
  Into Abdullah Bulbul Amir.

"Young man," said Bulbul, "is existence so dull
  That you're anxious to end your career?
Then, infidel, know you have trod on the toe
  Of Abdullah Bulbul Amir.

"So take your last look at the sea, sky and brook,
  Make your latest report on the war;
For I mean to imply you are going to die,
  O Ivan Petrofsky Skovar."

So this fierce man he took his trusty chibouk,
  And murmuring, "Allah Akbar!"
With murder intent he most savagely went
  For Ivan Petrofsky Skovar.

194

The Sultan rose up, the disturbance to quell,
  Likewise, give the victor a cheer.
He arrived just in time to bid hasty farewell
  To Abdullah Bulbul Amir.

A loud-sounding splash from the Danube was heard
  Resounding o'er meadows afar;
It came from the sack fitting close to the back
  Of Ivan Petrofsky Skovar.

There lieth a stone where the Danube doth roll,
  And on it in characters queer
Is "Stranger, when passing by, pray for the soul
  Of Abdullah Bulbul Amir."

A Muscovite maiden her lone vigil keeps
  By the light of the pale northern star,
And the name that she murmurs so oft as she weeps
  Is Ivan Petrofsky Skovar.

American song

THE BLAST OF WAR

from **King Henry V**

Act III, Scene 1

Once more unto the breach, dear friends, once more;
Or close the wall up with our English dead.
In peace there's nothing so becomes a man
As modest stillness and humility:
But when the blast of war blows in our ears,
Then imitate the action of the tiger;
Stiffen the sinews, summon up the blood,
Disguise fair nature with hard-favor'd rage;
Then lend the eye a terrible aspect;
Let it pry through the portage of the head
Like the brass cannon; let the brow o'erwhelm it
As fearfully as doth a galled rock
O'erhang and jutty his confounded base,
Swill'd with the wild and wasteful ocean.
Now set the teeth and stretch the nostril wide,
Hold hard the breath and bend up every spirit
To his full height. On, on, you noblest English,
Whose blood is fet from fathers of war-proof!
Fathers that, like so many Alexanders,
Have in these parts from morn till even fought,
And sheathed their swords for lack of argument:
Dishonor not your mothers; now attest
That those whom you call'd fathers did beget you.

Be copy now to men of grosser blood,
And teach them how to war. And you, good yeomen,
Whose limbs were made in England, show us here
The mettle of your pasture; let us swear
That you are worth your breeding; which I doubt not;
For there is none of you so mean and base,
That hath not noble luster in your eyes.
I see you stand like greyhounds in the slips,
Straining upon the start. The game's afoot:
Follow your spirit, and upon this charge
Cry "God for Harry, England, and Saint George!"

Act iv, Scene iii

. . . He which hath no stomach to this fight,
Let him depart; his passport shall be made
And crowns for convoy put into his purse:
We would not die in that man's company
That fears his fellowship to die with us.
This day is call'd the feast of Crispian:
He that outlives this day, and comes safe home,
Will stand a tip-toe when this day is named,
And rouse him at the name of Crispian.
He that shall live this day, and see old age,
Will yearly on the vigil feast his neighbors,
And say, "Tomorrow is Saint Crispian":
Then will he strip his sleeve and show his scars,
And say, "These wounds I had on Crispin's day."
Old men forget; yet all shall be forgot,
But he'll remember with advantages
What feats he did that day: then shall our names,
Familiar in his mouth as household words,
Harry the king, Bedford and Exeter,

Warwick and Talbot, Salisbury and Gloucester,
Be in their flowing cups freshly remember'd.
This story shall the good man teach his son;
And Crispin Crispian shall ne'er go by,
From this day to the ending of the world,
But we in it shall be rememberèd;
We few, we happy few, we band of brothers;
For he today that sheds his blood with me
Shall be my brother; be he ne'er so vile,
This day shall gentle his condition:
And gentlemen in England now a-bed
Shall think themselves accursed they were not here,
And hold their manhoods cheap whiles any speaks
That fought with us upon Saint Crispin's day.

William Shakespeare

The Captain

Then cam Lungeus with a spere
  And clift his hart in sonder.

Slowly he rode home at the end of day
  Over the plain toward the silken tent.
With shield and helmet hacked and surcoat rent
  Homeward the Captain rode. The air was gray,

The courser stumbled in the sword-strewn way,
  The broken-toothed and shattered battlement
Towered with vacant grinning as he went
  Home from the fight in triumph and dismay.

His wounded side still bled. The stars were pale.
  Beyond the blackened wall, against his orders,
Busy lieutenants hanged the caught marauders,
  Felon and mutineer and beaten foeman.
The aching Captain in his coat of mail
  Sought his pavilion sobbing like a woman.

Jon Manchip White

Carentan O Carentan

Trees in the old days used to stand
And shape a shady lane
Where lovers wandered hand in hand
Who came from Carentan.

This was the shining green canal
Where we came two by two
Walking at combat interval.
Such trees we never knew.

The day was early June, the ground
Was soft and bright with dew.
Far away the guns did sound,
But here the sky was blue.

The sky was blue, but there a smoke
Hung still above the sea
Where the ships together spoke
To towns we could not see.

Could you have seen us through a glass
You would have said a walk
Of farmers out to turn the grass,
Each with his own hayfork.

The watchers in their leopard suits
Waited till it was time,
And aimed between the belt and boot
And let the barrel climb.

I must lie down at once, there is
A hammer at my knee.
And call it death or cowardice,
Don't count again on me.

Everything's all right, Mother,
Everyone gets the same
At one time or another.
It's all in the game.

I never strolled, nor ever shall,
Down such a leafy lane.
I never drank in a canal,
Nor ever shall again.

There is a whistling in the leaves
And it is not the wind,
The twigs are falling from the knives
That cut men to the ground.

Tell me, Master Sergeant,
The way to turn and shoot.
But the Sergeant's silent
That taught me how to do it.

O Captain, show us quickly
Our place upon the map.
But the Captain's sickly
And taking a long nap.

Lieutenant, what's my duty,
My place in the platoon?
He too's a sleeping beauty,
Charmed by that strange tune.

Carentan O Carentan
Before we met with you
We never yet had lost a man
Or known what death could do.

Louis Simpson

Counter-Attack

We'd gained our first objective hours before
While dawn broke like a face with blinking eyes,
Pallid, unshaved and thirsty, blind with smoke.
Things seemed all right at first. We held their line,
With bombers posted, Lewis guns well placed,
And clink of shovels deepening the shallow trench.
   The place was rotten with dead; green clumsy legs
   High-booted, sprawled and groveled along the saps,
   And trunks, face downward, in the sucking mud,
   Wallowed like trodden sandbags loosely filled;
   And naked sodden buttocks, mats of hair,
   Bulged, clotted heads slept in the plastering slime.
   And then the rain began—the jolly old rain!

A yawning soldier knelt against the bank,
Staring across the morning blear with fog;
He wondered when the Allemands would get busy;
And then, of course, they started with five-nines
Traversing, sure as fate, and never a dud.

204

Mute in the clamor of shells he watched them burst
Spouting dark earth and wire with gusts from hell,
While posturing giants dissolved in drifts of smoke.
He crouched and flinched, dizzy with galloping fear,
Sick for escape—loathing the strangled horror
And butchered, frantic gestures of the dead.

An officer came blundering down the trench:
"Stand to and man the fire step!" On he went . . .
Gasping and bawling, "Fire step . . . counter-attack!"
   Then the haze lifted. Bombing on the right
   Down the old sap: machine guns on the left;
   And stumbling figures looming out in front.
   "O Christ, they're coming at us!" Bullets spat,
And he remembered his rifle . . . rapid fire . . .
And started blazing wildly . . . then a bang
Crumpled and spun him sideways, knocked him out
To grunt and wriggle: none heeded him; he choked
And fought the flapping veils of smothering gloom,
Lost in a blurred confusion of yells and groans . . .
Down, and down, and down, he sank and drowned,
Bleeding to death. The counter-attack had failed.

Siegfried Sassoon

The Bonnie Earl of Moray

Ye Highlands and ye Lawlands,
   Oh! where hae ye been?
They hae slain the Earl of Moray,
   And hae laid him on the green.

Now wae be to thee, Huntly,
   And wherefore did you sae?
I bade you bring him wi' you,
   But forbade you him to slay.

He was a braw gallant,
   And he rid at the ring;
And the bonnie Earl of Moray,
   Oh! he might hae been a king.

He was a braw gallant,
   And he played at the ba';
And the bonnie Earl of Moray
   Was the flower amang them a'.

He was a braw gallant,
   And he played at the glove;
And the bonnie Earl of Moray,
   Oh! he was the Queen's luve.

Oh! lang will his lady
   Look owre the castle Doune,
Ere she see the Earl of Moray
   Come sounding thro' the toun.

Scottish folk song

A Kind of Hero

At school he was revered, yet lonely.
No other boy, however much
He might dream of it,
Dared to try to be his friend.
He walked, gaunt and piratical,
All bones and grin,
Towards his inescapable end.

Revered, but not by authority,
He poured ink into the new hat
Of the French master,
Painted the blackboard white,
Swore at the huge Principal,
Refused to bend
And invited him to a free fight.

In memory he is beautiful,
But only his desperate gold
Hair might have been so.
Vaguely we understood,
And were grateful, that he performed
Our lawless deeds;
Punished, he allowed us to be good.

The end: he was killed at Alamein.
He wore handcuffs on the troopship
Going out, his webbing
All scrubbed as white as rice;
And we, or others like us,
Were promoted
By his last derisive sacrifice.

Vernon Scannell

The Hero

"Jack fell as he'd have wished," the Mother said,
And folded up the letter that she'd read.
"The Colonel writes so nicely." Something broke
In the tired voice that quavered to a choke.
She half looked up. "We mothers are so proud
Of our dead soldiers." Then her face was bowed.

Quietly the Brother Officer went out.
He'd told the poor old dear some gallant lies
That she would nourish all her days, no doubt.
For while he coughed and mumbled, her weak eyes
Had shone with gentle triumph, brimmed with joy,
Because he'd been so brave, her glorious boy.

He thought how Jack, cold-footed, useless swine,
Had panicked down the trench that night the mine
Went up at Wicked Corner; how he'd tried
To get sent home; and how, at last, he died,
Blown to small bits. And no one seemed to care
Except that lonely woman with white hair.

Siegfried Sassoon

The Rebel

Oh, I'm a good old rebel, that's what I am,
And for this land of freedom, I don't give a damn;
I'm glad I fought agin her, I only wish we'd won,
And I ain't axed any pardon for anything I've done.

I fought with old Bob Lee for three years about,
Got wounded in four places and starved at Point Lookout.
I caught the rheumatism a-campin' in the snow,
And I killed a chance of Yankees and I wish I'd killed
    some mo'!

Three hundred thousand Yankees is dead in Southern dust,
We got three hundred thousand before they conquered us;
They died of Southern fever, of Southern steel and shot—
I wish they was three million instead of what we got.

I hate the Constitution, this great republic, too;
I hate the nasty eagle, and the uniform so blue;
I hate their glorious banner, and all their flags and fuss.
Those lying, thieving Yankees, I hate 'em wuss and wuss.

I hate the Yankee nation and everything they do;
I hate the Declaration of Independence too;
I hate the glorious Union, 'tis dripping with our blood;
I hate the striped banner, I fought it all I could.

I won't be reconstructed! I'm better now than them;
And for a carpetbagger, I don't give a damn;
So I'm off for the frontier, soon as I can go,
I'll prepare me a weapon and start for Mexico.

I can't take up my musket and fight them now no mo',
But I'm not goin' to love 'em, and that is certain sho';
And I don't want no pardon for what I was or am,
I won't be reconstructed and I don't give a damn.

Innes Randolph

Conquerors

By sundown we came to a hidden village
Where all the air was still
And no sound met our tired ears, save
For the sorry drip of rain from blackened trees
And the melancholy song of swinging gates.
Then through a broken pane some of us saw
A dead bird in a rusting cage, still
Pressing his thin tattered breast against the bars,
His beak wide open. And
As we hurried through the weed-grown street,
A gaunt dog started up from some dark place
And shambled off on legs as thin as sticks
Into the wood, to die at least in peace.
No one had told us victory was like this;
Not one amongst us would have eaten bread
Before he'd filled the mouth of the gray child
That sprawled, stiff as a stone, before the shattered door.
There was not one who did not think of home.

Henry Treece

Dulce et Decorum Est

Bent double, like old beggars under sacks,
Knock-kneed, coughing like hags, we cursed through
    sludge,
Till on the haunting flares we turned our backs,
And towards our distant rest began to trudge.
Men marched asleep. Many had lost their boots,
But limped on, blood-shod. All went lame, all blind;

Drunk with fatigue; deaf even to the hoots
Of gas shells dropping softly behind.
Gas! GAS! Quick, boys—An ecstasy of fumbling,
Fitting the clumsy helmets just in time,
But someone still was yelling out and stumbling
And floundering like a man in fire or lime.
Dim through the misty panes and thick green light,
As under a green sea, I saw him drowning.

In all my dreams before my helpless sight
He plunges at me, guttering, choking, drowning.

If in some smothering dreams, you too could pace
Behind the wagon that we flung him in,
And watch the white eyes writhing in his face,
His hanging face, like a devil's sick of sin;
If you could hear, at every jolt, the blood
Come gargling from the froth-corrupted lungs,
Bitter as the cud
Of vile, incurable sores on innocent tongues,
My friend, you would not tell with such high zest
To children ardent for some desperate glory,
The old Lie: Dulce et decorum est
Pro patria mori.

Wilfred Owen

Andrew Jackson

He was a man as hot as whisky.
He was a man whose word was good.
He was a man whose hate was risky—
  Andrew Jackson—hickory wood!

He was in love with love and glory:
His hopes were prospered, but at a price—
The bandying of the ugly story
  He'd had to marry his Rachel twice.

Hot he was and a hasty suitor,
But if he sinned he was poor at sin.
She was plain as a spoon of pewter,
  Plain and good as a safety pin.

Andrew Jackson, man of honor,
Held her name like he held his head.
He stopped a bullet for slurs upon her.
  All his life he carried lead.

All his life wherever he went he
Wore the scar of a pistol shot—
Along with others he had in plenty.
  Hickory wood is hard to rot.

Hard to rot and a fiery fuel—
When faith and freedom both burned dim,
He stood his guns as he fought a duel,
  And heartened others to stand with him.

With any man who was good at sighting,
No ally but the thief Lafitte,
And no campaigns but Indian fighting—
    He brought the British to black defeat.

The odds against him were more than double.
His gun mounts sank like a heart that fails,
Sank in mud and the frosty stubble—
    So he set his cannon on cotton bales.

And over the cane and the silver sedges—
The redcoats' coats were as red as flame—
In a hundred rows like a hundred hedges,
    The bayonets of the British came.

The smoke of his cannon rolled and scattered
Like bursting flowers, like cotton blooms.
Like teeth from a comb the red ranks shattered,
    While water lifted in yellow plumes.

White and red on the silver carpet,
Scarlet tunics by crossbelts crossed,
They fell and died—and a flood of scarlet
    Covered over the field of frost.

He was a man whose hand was steady.
He was a man whose aim was good.
He was a man whose guns were ready—
    Andrew Jackson—hickory wood!

                        Martha Keller

Bill 'Awkins

" 'As anybody seen Bill 'Awkins?"
    "Now 'ow in the devil would I know?"
" 'E's taken my girl out walkin',
    An' I've got to tell 'im so—
        Gawd—bless—'im!
    I've got to tell 'im so."

"D'yer know what 'e's like, Bill 'Awkins?"
    "Now what in the devil would I care?"
" 'E's the livin', breathin' image of an organ-grinder's
        monkey,
    With a pound of grease in 'is 'air—
        Gawd—bless—'im!
    An' a pound o' grease in 'is 'air."

"An' s'pose you met Bill 'Awkins,
    Now what in the devil 'ud ye do?"
"I'd open 'is cheek to 'is chin-strap buckle,
    An' bung up 'is both eyes, too—
        Gawd—bless—'im!
    An' bung up 'is both eyes, too!"

"Look 'ere, where 'e comes, Bill 'Awkins!
    Now what in the devil will you say?"
"It isn't fit an' proper to be fightin' on a Sunday,
    So I'll pass 'im the time o' day—
        Gawd—bless—'im!
    I'll pass 'im the time o' day!"

Rudyard Kipling

On a Portrait by Copley

The General requires a portrait;
Copley is at length engaged
to represent, with art and passion,
Mars, the bellicose, enraged.

His countenance, conflagratory,
speaks of fire, and smoke, and war.
His gaze, he says, goes forward with
"That freedom I have foughten for."

So let his eye be falcon-sharp—
let every grizzly sinew tense
into the rigid pose. "I say
attack! The *devil* with defense!"

And for effect, a cannon at
the canvas border. "War is Hell. . . ."
A flag to furl above him. "Yet,
I served my country long and well."

Is *Copley* taken in? Not quite.
We see a ruddy windbag, whose
combustious face and eyes are bright
with apoplexy, bulk, and booze.

Arthur Freeman

Soldier's Song

I sing the praise of honored wars,
The glory of well-gotten scars,
The bravery of glittering shields,
Of lusty hearts and famous fields;
For that is music worth the ear of Jove,
A sight for kings, and still the soldier's love.

Look! Oh, methinks I see
The grace of chivalry;
The colors are displayed,
The captains bright arrayed.
See now the battle's ranged,
Bullets now thick are changed.
Hark! shots and wounds abound,
The drums alarum sound.
The captains cry: Za-za!
The trumpets sound ta-ra!
Oh, this is music worth the ear of Jove,
A sight for kings, and still the soldier's love.

Tobias Hume

Mules

I never would 'ave done it if I'd known what it would be.
I thought it meant promotion an' some extra pay for me;
I thought I'd miss a drill or two with packs an' trenchin'
    tools,
So I said I'd 'andled 'orses—an' they set me 'andlin' mules.

216

Now 'orses they are 'orses, but a mule 'e is a mule
(Bit o' devil, bit o' monkey, bit o' bloomin' boundin' fool!).
Oh, I'm usin' all the adjectives I didn't learn at school
On the prancin', glancin', ragtime dancin' Army Transport
   mule.

If I'd been Father Noah when the cargo walked aboard,
I'd 'ave let the bears an' tigers in, an' never spoke a word;
But I'd 'ave shoved a placard out to say the 'ouse was full,
An' shut the Ark up suddent when I saw the Army mule.

They buck you off when ridden, they squish your leg when
   led,
They're mostly sittin' on their tail or standin' on their
   'ead;
They reach their yellow grinders out an' gently chew your
   ear,
An' their necks is India rubber for attackin' in the rear.

They're as mincin' when they're 'appy as a ladies' ridin'
   school,
But when the fancy takes 'em they're like nothin' but a
   mule—
With the off wheels in the gutter an' the near wheels in the
   air,
An' a leg across the traces, an' the driver Lord knows
   where.

They're 'orrid in the stable, they're worse upon the road;
They'll bolt with any rider, they'll jib with any load;
But soon we're bound beyond the seas, an' when we cross
   the foam
I don't care where we go to if we leave the mules at 'ome.

For 'orses they are 'orses, but a mule 'e is a mule
(Bit o' devil, bit o' monkey, bit o' bloomin' boundin' fool!).
Oh, I'm usin' all the adjectives I never learned at school
On the rampin', rawboned, cast-steel-jawboned Army
   Transport mule.

C. Fox Smith

The Man He Killed

"Had he and I but met
  By some old ancient inn,
We should have sat us down to wet
  Right many a nipperkin!

"But ranged as infantry,
  And staring face to face,
I shot at him as he at me,
  And killed him in his place.

"I shot him dead because—
  Because he was my foe,
Just so: my foe of course he was;
  That's clear enough; although

"He thought he'd 'list, perhaps,
  Offhand-like—just as I—
Was out of work—had sold his traps—
  No other reason why.

"Yes; quaint and curious war is!
  You shoot a fellow down
You'd treat if met where any bar is,
  Or help to half a crown."

Thomas Hardy

Death and General Putnam

His iron arm had spent its force,
No longer might he rein a horse;
Lone, beside the dying blaze
Dreaming dreams of younger days
   Sat old Israel Putnam.

Twice he heard, then three times more
A knock upon the oaken door,
A knock he could not fail to know,
That old man in the ember-glow.
   "Come," said General Putnam.

The door swung wide; in cloak and hood
Lean and tall the pilgrim stood
And spoke in tones none else might hear,
"Once more I come to bring you Fear!"
   "Fear?" said General Putnam.

"You know not Fear? And yet this face
Your eyes have seen in many a place
Since first in stony Pomfret, when
You dragged the mad wolf from her den."
   "Yes," said General Putnam.

"Was I not close, when, stripped and bound
With blazing fagots heaped around
You heard the Huron war cry shrill?
Was I not close at Bunker Hill?"
   "Close," said General Putnam.

"Am I not that which strong men dread
On stricken field or fevered bed
On gloomy trail and stormy sea,
And dare you name my name to me?"
　　"Death," said General Putnam.

"We have been comrades, you and I,
In chase and war beneath this sky;
And now, whatever Fate may send,
Old comrade, can you call me friend?"
　　"Friend!" said General Putnam.

Then up he rose, and forth they went
Away from battleground, fortress, tent,
Mountain, wilderness, field and farm,
Death and the General, arm in arm,
　　Death and General Putnam.

　　　　　　　　　　Arthur Guiterman

Sergeant-Major Money
(1917)

It wasn't our battalion, but we lay alongside it,
　　So the story is as true as the telling is frank.
They hadn't one Line-officer left, after Arras,
　　Except a batty major and the Colonel, who drank.

"B" Company Commander was fresh from the Depot,
　　An expert on gas drill, otherwise a dud;
So Sergeant-Major Money carried on, as instructed,
　　And that's where the swaddies began to sweat blood.

220

His Old Army humor was so well spiced and hearty
    That one poor sod shot himself, and one lost his wits;
But discipline's maintained, and back in rest billets
    The Colonel congratulates "B" company on their kits.

The subalterns went easy, as was only natural
    With a terror like Money driving the machine,
Till finally two Welshmen, butties from the Rhondda,
    Bayoneted their bugbear in a field canteen.

Well, we couldn't blame the officers, they relied on Money;
    We couldn't blame the pitboys, their courage was grand;
Or, least of all, blame Money, an old stiff surviving
    In a New (bloody) Army he couldn't understand.

Robert Graves

The Messages

"I cannot quite remember. . . . There were five
Dropped dead beside me in the trench—and three
Whispered their dying messages to me. . . ."

Back from the trenches, more dead than alive,
Stone-deaf and dazed, and with a broken knee,
He hobbled slowly, muttering vacantly:

"I cannot quite remember. . . . There were five
Dropped dead beside me in the trench, and three
Whispered their dying messages to me. . . .

"Their friends are waiting, wondering how they thrive—
Waiting a word in silence patiently. . . .
But what they said, or who their friends may be

"I cannot quite remember. . . . There were five
Dropped dead beside me in the trench—and three
Whispered their dying messages to me. . . ."

W. W. Gibson

INDEPENDENT SPIRITS

John Henry

When John Henry was a little baby,
Sitting on his papa's knee,
Well, he picked up a hammer and a little piece of steel,
Said, "Hammer's gonna be the death of me, Lord, Lord!
Hammer's gonna be the death of me."

The captain said to John Henry,
"I'm gonna bring that steam drill around,
I'm gonna bring that steam drill out on the job,
I'm gonna whup that steel on down, Lord, Lord!
Whup that steel on down."

John Henry told his captain,
"Lord, a man ain't nothing but a man,
But before I'd let your steam drill beat me down,
I'd die with a hammer in my hand, Lord, Lord!
Die with a hammer in my hand."

John Henry said to his shaker,
"Shaker, why don't you sing?
Because I'm swinging thirty pounds from my hips on down;
Just listen to that cold steel ring, Lord, Lord!
Listen to that cold steel ring."

Now, the captain said to John Henry,
"I believe that mountain's caving in."
John Henry said right back to the captain,
"Ain't nothing but my hammer catching wind, Lord Lord!
Nothing but my hammer catching wind."

Now, the man that invented the steam drill,
He thought he was mighty fine;
But John Henry drove fifteen feet,
The steam drill only made nine, Lord, Lord!
Steam drill only made nine.

John Henry hammered in the mountains,
His hammer was striking fire,
But he worked so hard it broke his poor heart
And he laid down his hammer and he died, Lord, Lord!
Laid down his hammer and he died.

Now, John Henry had a little woman,
Her name was Polly Anne,
John Henry took sick and had to go to bed,
Polly Anne drove steel like a man, Lord, Lord!
Polly Anne drove steel like a man.

John Henry had a little baby,
You could hold him in the palm of your hand;
And the last words I heard that poor boy say,
"My daddy was a steel-driving man, Lord, Lord!
My daddy was a steel-driving man."

So every Monday morning
When the bluebirds begin to sing,
You can hear John Henry a mile or more;
You can hear John Henry's hammer ring, Lord, Lord!
Hear John Henry's hammer ring.

American ballad

The Village Burglar

Under a spreading gooseberry bush the village burglar lies;
The burglar is a hairy man with whiskers round his eyes
And the muscles of his brawny arms keep off the little flies.
He goes on Sunday to the church to hear the Parson shout;
He puts a penny in the plate and takes a pound note out,
And drops a conscience-stricken tear in case he is found
 out.

Anonymous

Juan Belmonte, Torero

The first thing, I think, is a keen sense
Of the ridiculous. Before each corrida
To finger anew one's duties, one's motivations,
A housewife among suspicious vegetables.
Outside the mob shifts on its terrible
Haunches. It is strange: without them,
The whole thing is meaningless. The bull
Has more sense of his part. Many times I sit
Out there: I think to myself, how the hell
Can he do it? I see the bull tear out
Of the toril, and I am convinced that I should
Never be able to fight him.
                              How much easier
In the old days. In Tablada, naked and dripping
Under the moon, losing the bull in the darkness;
Then suddenly the white horns, like the arms
Of a bathing girl.

Each time they expected
More, and each time I had less to give.
Now I no longer remember what it was that
I *meant* to give. The mob shakes its terrible
Hair. The old faenas are smoothed into
The sand. Glittering young men tread on it,
In their soft slippers and their bravery.

Donald Finkel

The Ballad of William Sycamore
(1790–1871)

My father, he was a mountaineer,
His fist was a knotty hammer;
He was quick on his feet as a running deer,
And he spoke with a Yankee stammer.

My mother, she was merry and brave,
And so she came to her labor,
With a tall green fir for her doctor grave
And a stream for her comforting neighbor.

And some are wrapped in the linen fine,
And some like a godling's scion;
But I was cradled on twigs of pine
In the skin of a mountain lion.

And some remember a white, starched lap
And an ewer with silver handles;
But I remember a coonskin cap
And the smell of bayberry candles,

The cabin logs, with the bark still rough,
And my mother, who laughed at trifles,

228

And the tall, lank visitors, brown as snuff,
With their long, straight squirrel rifles.

I can hear them dance, like a foggy song,
Through the deepest one of my slumbers,
The fiddle squeaking the boots along,
And my father calling the numbers;

The quick feet shaking the puncheon floor,
And the fiddle squeaking and squealing,
Till the dried herbs rattled above the door
And the dust went up to the ceiling.

There are children lucky from dawn till dusk,
But never a child so lucky!
For I cut my teeth on "Money Musk"
In the Bloody Ground of Kentucky!

When I grew tall as the Indian corn,
My father had little to lend me,
But he gave me his great old powderhorn
And his woodsman's skill to befriend me.

With a leather shirt to cover my back,
And a redskin nose to unravel
Each forest sign, I carried my pack
As far as a scout could travel.

Till I lost my boyhood and found my wife,
A girl like a Salem clipper!
A woman straight as a hunting knife
With eyes as bright as the Dipper!

We cleared our camp where the buffalo feed,
Unheard-of streams were our flagons;

And I sowed my sons like the apple seed
On the trail of the Western wagons.

They were right, tight boys, never sulky or slow,
A fruitful, a goodly muster.
The eldest died at the Alamo;
The youngest fell with Custer.

The letter that told it burned my hand.
Yet we smiled and said, "So be it!"
But I could not live when they fenced the land,
For it broke my heart to see it.

I saddled a red, unbroken colt
And rode him into the day there;
And he threw me down like a thunderbolt
And rolled on me as I lay there.

The hunter's whistle hummed in my ear
As the city men tried to move me,
And I died in my boots like a pioneer
With the whole wide sky above me.

Now I lie in the heart of the fat, black soil,
Like the seed of a prairie thistle;
It has washed my bones with honey and oil
And picked them clean as a whistle.

And my youth returns, like the rains of Spring,
And my sons, like the wild geese flying;
And I lie and hear the meadowlark sing,
And I have much content in my dying.

Go play with the towns you have built of blocks,
The towns where you would have bound me!
I sleep in the earth like a tired fox,
And my buffalo have found me.

Stephen Vincent Benét

Peerless Jim Driscoll

I saw Jim Driscoll fight in nineteen-ten.
That takes you back a bit. You don't see men
Like Driscoll any more. The breed's died out.
There's no one fit to lace his boots about.
All right, son. Have your laugh. You know it all.
You think these mugs today that cuff and maul
Their way through ten or fifteen threes can fight:
They hardly know their left hand from their right.
But Jim, he knew: he never slapped or swung,
His left hand flickered like a cobra's tongue
And when he followed with the old one-two
Black lightning of those fists would dazzle you.
By Jesus he could hit. I've never seen
A sweeter puncher: every blow as clean
As silver. *Peerless Jim* the papers named him,
And yet he never swaggered, never bragged.
I saw him once when he got properly tagged—
A sucker punch from nowhere on the chin—
And he was hurt; but all he did was grin
And nod as if to say, "I asked for that."
No one was ever more worth looking at;
Up there beneath the ache of arc lamps he
Was just like what we'd love our sons to be
Or like those gods you've heard about at school. . . .
Well, yes, I'm old; and maybe I'm a fool.

I only saw him once outside the ring
And I admit I found it disappointing.
He looked just—I don't know—just ordinary,
And smaller, too, than what I thought he'd be:
An ordinary man in fact, like you or me.

Vernon Scannell

The Buffalo Skinners

'Twas in the town of Jacksboro in the spring of seventy-
    three,
A man by the name of Crego came stepping up to me,
Saying, "How do you do, young fellow, and how would
    you like to go
And spend the summer pleasantly on the range of the
    buffalo?"

And me not having any job, to old Crego I did say,
"This going out on the buffalo range depends upon the
    pay.
But if you will pay good wages, give transportation too,
I think that I will go with you to the range of the buffalo."

"Yes, I will pay good wages, give transportation too,
Provided you will go with me and stay the summer through;
But if you should grow homesick, come back to Jacksboro,
I won't pay transportation from the range of the buffalo."

Our meat it was of buffalo hump, like iron was our bread,
And all we had to sleep on was a buffalo for a bed;
The fleas and graybacks [1] worked on us, and boys, they
    were not slow;

[1] *graybacks:* lice

232

I tell you there's no worse hell on earth than the range of
the buffalo.

Our hearts were cased with buffalo hocks, our souls were
cased with steel;
The hardships of that summer would nearly make us reel.
While skinning the damned old stinkers, our lives they had
no show
For the Indians waited to pick us off on the hills of Mexico.

The season being over, old Crego he did say
The crowd had been extravagant, was in debt to him that
day.
We coaxed him and we begged him and still it was no go—
We left old Crego's bones to bleach on the range of the
buffalo.

It's now we've crossed Pease River and homeward we are
bound.
No more in that hell-fired country shall ever we be found;
Go home to our wives and sweethearts, tell others not to go.
For God's forsaken the buffalo range and the damned old
buffalo.

American folk ballad

Reuben Bright

Because he was a butcher and thereby
Did earn an honest living (and did right),
I would not have you think that Reuben Bright
Was any more a brute than you or I;
For when they told him that his wife must die,
He stared at them, and shook with grief and fright,

And cried like a great baby half that night,
And made the women cry to see him cry.

And after she was dead, and he had paid
The singers and the sexton and the rest,
He packed a lot of things that she had made
Most mournfully away in an old chest
Of hers, and put some chopped-up cedar boughs
In with them, and tore down the slaughterhouse.

Edwin Arlington Robinson

Jim Bludso

Wal, no! I can't tell whar he lives,
   Because he don't live, you see;
Leastways, he's got out of the habit
   Of livin' like you and me.
Where have you been for the last three years
   That you haven't heard folks tell
How Jemmy Bludso passed in his checks,
   The night of the Prairie Belle?

He weren't no saint—them engineers
   Is all pretty much alike—
One wife in Natchez-under-the-Hill,
   And another one here in Pike.
A keerless man in his talk was Jim,
   And an awkward man in a row—
But he never flunked, and he never lied;
   I reckon he never knowed how.

And this was all the religion he had—
   To treat his engines well;

Never be passed on the river;
  To mind the pilot's bell;
And if ever the Prairie Belle took fire,
  A thousand times he swore,
He'd hold her nozzle agin the bank
  Till the last soul got ashore.

All boats have their day on the Mississip,
  And her day come at last.
The Movastar was a better boat,
  But the Belle she wouldn't be passed;
And so come tearin' along that night,—
  The oldest craft on the line,
With a stoker squat on her safety valve,
  And her furnace crammed, rosin and pine.

The fire bust out as she clared the bar,
  And burnt a hole in the night,
And quick as a flash she turned, and made
  To that willer-bank on the right.
There was runnin' and cursin', but Jim yelled out
  Over all the infernal roar,
"I'll hold her nozzle agin the bank
  Till the last galoot's ashore."

Through the hot black breath of the burnin' boat
  Jim Bludso's voice was heard,
And they all had trust in his cussedness,
  And knowed he would keep his word.
And, sure's you're born, they all got off
  Afore the smokestacks fell,—
And Bludso's ghost went up alone
  In the smoke of the Prairie Belle.

He weren't no saint—but at jedgment
   I'd run my chance with Jim,
'Longside of some pious gentlemen
   That wouldn't shook hands with him.
He'd seen his duty, a dead-sure thing—
   And went for it thar and then:
And Christ ain't a-going to be too hard
   On a man that died for men.

                              John Hay

The Ox Tamer

In a faraway northern county in the placid pastoral region,
Lives my farmer friend, the theme of my recitative, a famous
   tamer of oxen,
There they bring him the three-year-olds and the four-year-
   olds to break them.
He will take the wildest steer in the world and break him
   and tame him.
He will go fearless without any whip where the young
   bullock chafes up and down the yard,
The bullock's head tosses restless high in the air with raging
   eyes.
Yet see you! how soon his rage subsides—how soon this
   tamer tames him;
See you! on the farms hereabout a hundred oxen young
   and old, and he is the man who has tamed them,
They all know him, all are affectionate to him;
See you! some are such beautiful animals, so lofty looking;
Some are buff-colored, some mottled, one has a white line
   running along his back, some are brindled,
Some have wide flaring horns (a good sign)—see you! the
   bright hides,

See, the two with stars on their foreheads—see, the round
    bodies and broad backs,
How straight and square they stand on their legs—what
    fine sagacious eyes!
How they watch their tamer—they wish him near them—
    how they turn to look after him!
What yearning expression! how uneasy they are when he
    moves away from them;
Now I marvel what it can be he appears to them (books,
    politics, poems, depart—all else departs),
I confess I envy only his fascination—my silent illiterate
    friend,
Whom a hundred oxen love there in his life on farms,
In the northern county far, in the placid pastoral region.

Walt Whitman

The Lincolnshire Poacher

When I was bound apprentice in famous Lincolnshire,
Full well I served my master for more than seven year,
Till I took up to poaching, as you shall quickly hear;
O 'tis my delight, on a shining night, in the season of the
    year.

As me and my companions were setting of a snare,
'Twas then we spied the gamekeeper; for him we did not
    care.
For we can wrestle and fight, my boys, and jump o'er
    anywhere.
O 'tis my delight, on a shining night, in the season of the
    year.

As me and my companions were setting four or five,
And taking on them up again we caught a hare alive;

We took the hare alive, my boys, and through the woods
   did steer.
O 'tis my delight, on a shining night, in the season of the
   year.

I threw him on my shoulder, and then we trudged home;
We took him to a neighbor's house, and sold him for a
   crown;
We sold him for a crown, my boys, but I did not tell you
   where.
O 'tis my delight, on a shining night, in the season of the
   year.

English folk song

Daniel

Darius the Mede was a king and a wonder.
His eye was proud, and his voice was thunder.   *Beginning*
He kept bad lions in a monstrous den.   *with a strain*
He fed up the lions on Christian men.   *of "Dixie."*

Daniel was the chief hired man of the land.
He stirred up the music in the palace band.
He whitewashed the cellar. He shoveled in   *With a*
   the coal.   *touch of*
And Daniel kept a-praying:—"Lord save my   *"Alexander's*
   soul."   *Ragtime Band."*
Daniel kept a-praying:—"Lord save my soul."
Daniel kept a-praying:—"Lord save my soul."

Daniel was the butler, swagger and swell.
He ran up stairs. He answered the bell.

238

And *he* would let in whoever came a-calling:—
Saints so holy, scamps so appalling.
"Old man Ahab leaves his card.
Elisha and the bears are a-waiting in the yard.
Here comes Pharaoh and his snakes a-calling.
Here comes Cain and his wife a-calling.
Shadrach, Meshach and Abednego for tea.
Here comes Jonah and the whale,
And the *Sea!*
Here comes St. Peter and his fishing pole.
Here comes Judas and his silver a-calling.
Here comes old Beelzebub a-calling."
And Daniel kept a-praying:—"Lord save my soul."
Daniel kept a-praying:—"Lord save my soul."
Daniel kept a-praying:—"Lord save my soul."

His sweetheart and his mother were Christian and meek.
They washed and ironed for Darius every week.
One Thursday he met them at the door:—
Paid them as usual, but acted sore.

He said:—"Your Daniel is a dead little pigeon.
He's a good hard worker, but he talks religion."
And he showed them Daniel in the lions' cage.
Daniel standing quietly, the lions in a rage.
His good old mother cried:—
"Lord save him."
And Daniel's tender sweetheart cried:—
"Lord save him."

And she was a golden lily in the dew. *This to be*
And she was as sweet as an apple on the tree, *repeated*
And she was as fine as a melon in the cornfield, *three times,*
Gliding and lovely as a ship on the sea, *very softly*
Gliding and lovely as a ship on the sea. *and slowly.*

239

And she prayed to the Lord:—
"Send Gabriel. Send Gabriel."

King Darius said to the lions:—
"Bite Daniel. Bite Daniel.
Bite him. Bite him. Bite him!"

Thus roared the lions:—   *Here the*
"We want Daniel, Daniel, Daniel,   *audience roars with*
We want Daniel, Daniel, Daniel."   *the leader.*

And Daniel did not frown,
Daniel did not cry.
He kept on looking at the sky.
And the Lord said to Gabriel:—   *The audience*
"Go chain the lions down.   *sings this*
Go chain the lions down.   *with the*
Go chain the lions down.   *leader, to the*
Go chain the lions down."   *old Negro tune.*

And *Gabriel* chained the lions,
And *Gabriel* chained the lions,
And *Gabriel* chained the lions,
And Daniel got out of the den,
And Daniel got out of the den,
And Daniel got out of the den.
And Darius said:—"You're a Christian child,"
Darius said:—"You're a Christian child,"
Darius said:—"You're a Christian child,"
And gave him his job again,
And gave him his job again,
And gave him his job again.

Vachel Lindsay

240

A Butcher

Whoe'er has gone thro' London Street,
Has seen a Butcher gazing at his meat,
    And how he keeps
    Gloating upon a sheep's
Or bullock's personals, as if his own;
    How he admires his halves
    And quarters—and his calves,
As if in truth upon his own legs grown;
    His fat! *his* suet!
His kidneys peeping elegantly thro' it!
    His thick flank!
    And *his* thin!
      His shank!
      His shin!
Skin of his skin, and bone too of his bone!

    With what an air
He stands aloof, across the thoroughfare
Gazing—and will not let a body by,
Tho' buy! buy! buy! be constantly his cry.
Meanwhile with arms akimbo, and a pair
Of Rhodian legs, he revels in a stare
At his Joint Stock—for one may call it so,
    Howbeit without a *Co.*
The dotage of self-love was never fonder
Than he of his brute bodies all a-row;
Narcissus in the wave did never ponder
    With love so strong,
    On his "portrait charmant,"
As our vain Butcher on his carcass yonder.

Look at his sleek round skull!
How bright his cheek, how rubicund his nose is!
    His visage seems to be
    Ripe for beef tea;
Of brutal juices the whole man is full.
In fact, fulfilling the metempsychosis,
The Butcher is already half a Bull.

                Thomas Hood

The Song of the Banana Man

Touris', white man, wipin' his face,
Met me in Golden Grove market place.
He looked at m' ol' clothes brown wid stain,
An' soaked right through wid de Portlan' rain,
He cas' his eye, turn' up his nose,
He says, "You're a beggar man, I suppose?"
He says, "Boy, get some occupation,
Be of some value to your nation."

I said, "By God and dis big right han'
You mus' recognize a banana man.

"Up in de hills, where de streams are cool,
An' mullet an' janga [1] swim in de pool,
I have ten acres of mountainside,
An' a dainty-foot donkey dat I ride,
Four Gros Michel,[2] an' four Lacatan,[2]
Some coconut trees, and some hills of yam,
An' I pasture on dat very same lan'
Five she-goats an' a big black ram,

[1] *janga*: a crayfish, found in some of the rivers of Jamaica
[2] *Gros Michel* (pronounced "grow mee-shell") and *Lacatan*: two
varieties of bananas

242

"Dat, by God an' dis big right han'
Is de property of a banana man.

"I leave m' yard early-mornin' time
An' set m' foot to de mountain climb,
I ben' m' back to de hot-sun toil,
An' m' cutlass rings on de stony soil,
Ploughin' an' weedin', diggin' an' plantin'
Till Massa Sun drop back o' John Crow mountain,
Den home again in cool evenin' time,
Perhaps whistling dis likkle rhyme,

(*Sung*) "Praise God an' m' big right han'
I will live an' die a banana man.

"Banana day is my special day,
I cut my stems an' I'm on m' way,
Load up de donkey, leave de lan'
Head down de hill to banana stan',
When de truck comes roun' I take a ride
All de way down to de harbor side—
Dat is de night, when you, touris' man,
Would change your place wid a banana man.

"Yes, by God, an' m' big right han'
I will live an' die a banana man.

"De bay is calm, an' de moon is bright
De hills look black for de sky is light,
Down at de dock is an English ship,
Restin' after her ocean trip,
While on de pier is a monstrous hustle,
Tallymen, carriers, all in a bustle,
Wid stems on deir heads in a long black snake
Some singin' de songs dat banana men make,

"Like, (*Sung*) Praise God an' m' big right han'
I will live an' die a banana man.

"Den de payment comes, an' we have some fun,
Me, Zekiel, Breda and Duppy Son.
Down at de bar near United Wharf
We knock back a white rum, bus' a laugh,
Fill de empty bag for further toil
Wid saltfish, breadfruit, coconut oil.
Den head back home to m' yard to sleep,
A proper sleep dat is long an' deep.

"Yes, by God, an' m' big right han'
I will live an' die a banana man.

"So when you see dese ol' clothes brown wid stain,
An' soaked right through wid de Portlan' rain,
Don't cas' your eye nor turn your nose,
Don't judge a man by his patchy clothes,
I'm a strong man, a proud man, an' I'm free,
Free as dese mountains, free as dis sea,
I know myself, an' I know my ways,
An' will sing wid pride to de end o' my days,

(*Sung*) "Praise God an' m' big right han'
I will live an' die a banana man."

Evan Jones

Invictus

Out of the night that covers me,
   Black as the pit from pole to pole,
I thank whatever gods may be
   For my unconquerable soul.

In the fell clutch of circumstance
   I have not winced nor cried aloud:
Under the bludgeonings of chance
   My head is bloody, but unbowed.

Beyond this place of wrath and tears
   Looms but the horror of the shade,
And yet the menace of the years
   Finds and shall find me unafraid.

It matters not how strait the gate,
   How charged with punishments the scroll,
I am the master of my fate:
   I am the captain of my soul.

William Ernest Henley

Index of Authors

Benét, Stephen Vincent
The Ballad of William Sycamore   228

Blight, John
Camp Fever   96

Burnet, Dana
The Sack of Old Panama   56

Casey, Thomas F.
Drill, Ye Tarriers, Drill   125

Cather, Willa
Spanish Johnny   26

Cato, Nancy
The Dead Swagman   140

Causley, Charles
Cowboy Song   27

Cawein, Madison
The Man Hunt   88

Clancy, Joseph P.
Boxer   185

Clarke, Joseph I. C.
The Fighting Race   111

Davenant, Sir William
Storm at Sea   41

Davis, H. L.
Proud Riders   24

Falstaff, Jake
The Dick Johnson Reel   14

Finkel, Donald
Juan Belmonte, Torero   227

Freeman, Arthur
On a Portrait by Copley   215

Gibson, W. W.
The Messages   221

Gilbert, W. S.
The Troubadour   75

Graves, Robert
1805   42
Sergeant-Major Money   220

Guiterman, Arthur
Death and General Putnam   219

Hardy, Thomas
The Man He Killed   218

Harrington, Edward
The Swagless Swaggie   148

Harte, Bret
The Society upon the Stanislaus   22

Hay, Clarence Leonard
Down and Out   151

Hay, John
Jim Bludso   234

Henley, William Ernest
Invictus   245

Holmes, Oliver Wendell
The Spectre Pig   103

Hood, Thomas
A Butcher   241

Howard, Dorothy
The Knifesmith   90

Hume, Tobias
Soldier's Song   216

Johnson, Burges
The Bashful Man   43

Jones, Evan
The Song of the Banana Man   242

Keller, Martha
Andrew Jackson   212

247

Kingsley, Charles
  The Last Buccaneer   60
  The Outlaw   161

Kinnell, Galway
  The Wolves   95

Kipling, Rudyard
  Bill 'Awkins   214
  Danny Deever   87
  Harp Song of the Dane Women   55
  The Lament of the Border Cattle Thief   159

Knibbs, Henry Herbert
  Charley Lee   172

Lindsay, Vachel
  Daniel   238
  Simon Legree—A Negro Sermon   182

Lueders, Edward
  Rodeo   24

Maginn, William
  The Irishman and the Lady   116

McGaffey, Ernest
  Geronimo   15

Michie, James
  Dooley Is a Traitor   119

Mitchell, Julian
  Lament for the Cowboy Life   21

Newbolt, Henry
  Admiral Death   62
  Admirals All   51

Newell, Robert Henry
  A Great Fight   179

Noyes, Alfred
  Saint George and the Dragon   82

Olson, Elder
  "Plot Improbable, Character Unsympathetic"   100

Owen, Wilfred
  Dulce et Decorum Est   210

Paramore, Edward E., Jr.
   The Ballad of Yukon Jake   133

Paterson, A. B. ("Banjo")
   The Man from Ironbark   146
   The Man from Snowy River   141

Pudney, John
   Ballad of the Long Drop   108

Randolph, Innes
   The Rebel   208

Robinson, Edward Arlington
   Reuben Bright   233

Root, E. Merrill
   Chicago Idyll   91

Rostand, Edmond
   Ballade (translated by Louis Untermeyer)   81

Rowlands, Samuel
   Sir Eglamour   80

Sassoon, Siegfried
   Counter-Attack   204
   The Hero   208

Scannell, Vernon
   A Kind of Hero   207
   First Fight   188
   Mastering the Craft   186
   Peerless Jim Driscoll   231

Service, Robert W.
   My Friends   137
   The Shooting of Dan McGrew   129

Shakespeare, William
   from *King Henry V*   199

Sill, Edward Rowland
   Opportunity   71

Silverstein, Shel
   The Hunter   97

Simpson, Louis
   Carentan O Carentan   202

Smith, G. Fox
Mules 216

Stephens, James
Seumas Beg 63

Swift, Jonathan
Clever Tom Clinch 175

Synge, John Millington
Danny 124

Tennyson, Alfred, Lord
Kate 73
Sir Galahad 78
The Revenge 45

Thompson, Maurice
A Flight Shot 72

Treece, Henry
Conquerors 210

Webster, H.
Street Gang 187

White, Jon Manchip
The Captain 201

Whitman, Walt
The Ox Tamer 236

Anonymous
Abdullah Bulbul Amir 193
Admiral Benbow 66
Arthur McBride 115
Billy the Kid 164
Bold O'Donahue 122
Brennan on the Moor 165
'Dobe Bill 31
Greer County 15
Hell in Texas 30
Inscription from a Convict's Cell 164
Jack Hall 99
Jim Jones 139
John Hardy 16
John Henry 225
Mush, Mush 113

Paddy Murphy	118
Robin Hood and Little John	167
Samuel Hall	98
Tarpauling Jacket	64
The Bonnie Earl of Moray	206
The Buffalo Skinners	232
The Bullwhacker	18
The Crocodile	65
The Deckhands	53
The Insult	20
The Lincolnshire Poacher	237
The Streets of Laredo	28
The Three Butchers	102
The Village Burglar	227
The Wild Colonial Boy	171
Tying a Knot in the Devil's Tail	35
Whisky Bill	13

Index of Titles

Abdullah Bulbul Amir, *American song* — 193
Admiral Benbow, *Anonymous* — 66
Admiral Death, *Newbolt* — 62
Admirals All, *Newbolt* — 51
Andrew Jackson, *Keller* — 212
Arthur McBride, *Irish folk song* — 115

Ballad of the Long Drop, *Pudney* — 108
Ballad of William Sycamore, The, *Benét* — 228
Ballad of Yukon Jake, The, *Paramore* — 133
Ballade (from *Cyrano de Bergerac*), *Rostand (Untermeyer,*
    translator) — 81
Bashful Man, The, *Johnson* — 43
Bill 'Awkins, *Kipling* — 214
Billy the Kid, *American ballad* — 164
Bold O'Donahue, *Irish folk song* — 122
Bonnie Earl of Moray, The, *Scottish folk song* — 206
Boxer, *Clancy* — 185
Brennan on the Moor, *Irish ballad* — 165
Buffalo Skinners, The, *American folk ballad* — 232
Bullwhacker, The, *American ballad* — 18
Butcher, A, *Hood* — 241

Camp Fever, *Blight* — 96
Captain, The, *White* — 201
Carentan O Carentan, *Simpson* — 202
Charley Lee, *Knibbs* — 172
Chicago Idyll, *Root* — 91
Clever Tom Clinch, *Swift* — 175
Conquerors, *Treece* — 210
Counter-Attack, *Sassoon* — 204
Cowboy Song, *Causley* — 27
Crocodile, The, *Anonymous* — 65

Daniel, *Lindsay* — 238

Danny, *Synge*   124
Danny Deever, *Kipling*   87
Dead Swagman, The, *Cato*   140
Death and General Putnam, *Guiterman*   219
Deckhands, The, *Anonymous*   53
'Dobe Bill, *American cowboy song*   31
Dick Johnson Reel, The, *Falstaff*   14
Dooley Is a Traitor, *Michie*   119
Down and Out, *Hay, Clarence Leonard*   151
Drill, Ye Tarriers, Drill, *Casey*   125
Dulce et Decorum Est, *Owen*   210

1805, *Graves*   42

Fighting Race, The, *Clarke*   111
First Fight, *Scannell*   188
Flight Shot, A, *Thompson*   72

Geronimo, *McGaffey*   15
Great Fight, A, *Newell*   179
Greer County, *Anonymous*   15

Harp Song of the Dane Women, *Kipling*   55
Hell in Texas, *Anonymous*   30
Hero, The, *Sassoon*   208
Hunter, The, *Silverstein*   97

Inscription from a Convict's Cell, *Anonymous*   164
Insult, The, *American cowboy ballad*   20
Invictus, *Henley*   245
Irishman and the Lady, The, *Maginn*   116

Jack Hall, *English folk ballad*   99
Jim Bludso, *Hay, John*   234
Jim Jones, *Anonymous*   139
John Hardy, *American ballad*   16
John Henry, *American ballad*   225
Juan Belmonte, Torero, *Finkel*   227

Kate, *Tennyson*   73
Kind of Hero, A, *Scannell*   207
King Henry V (Excerpts), *Shakespeare*   199

Knifesmith, The, *Howard*   90

Lament of the Border Cattle Thief, The, *Kipling*   159
Lament for the Cowboy Life, *Mitchell*   21
Last Buccaneer, The, *Kingsley*   60
Lincolnshire Poacher, The, *English folk song*   237

Man from Ironbark, The, *Paterson*   146
Man from Snowy River, The, *Paterson*   141
Man He Killed, The, *Hardy*   218
Man Hunt, The, *Cawein*   88
Mastering the Craft, *Scannell*   186
Messages, The, *Gibson*   221
Mules, *Smith*   216
Mush, Mush, *Irish music-hall song*   113
My Friends, *Service*   137

On a Portrait by Copley, *Freeman*   215
Opportunity, *Sill*   71
Outlaw, The, *Kingsley*   161
Ox Tamer, The, *Whitman*   236

Paddy Murphy, *Anonymous*   118
Peerless Jim Driscoll, *Scannell*   231
"Plot Improbable, Character Unsympathetic," *Olson*   100
Proud Riders, *Davis*   24

Rebel, The, *Randolph*   208
Reuben Bright, *Robinson*   233
Revenge, The, *Tennyson*   45
Robin Hood and Little John, *English folk ballad*   167
Rodeo, *Lueders*   24

Sack of Old Panama, The, *Burnet*   56
Saint George and the Dragon, *Noyes*   82
Samuel Hall, *American folk ballad*   98
Seumas Beg, *Stephens*   63
Sergeant-Major Money, *Graves*   220
Shooting of Dan McGrew, The, *Service*   129
Simon Legree—A Negro Sermon, *Lindsay*   182
Sir Eglamour, *Rowlands*   80
Sir Galahad, *Tennyson*   78

Society upon the Stanislaus, The, *Harte*   22
Soldier's Song, *Hume*   216
Song of the Banana Man, The, *Jones*   242
Spanish Johnny, *Cather*   26
Spectre Pig, The, *Holmes*   103
Storm at Sea, *Davenant*   41
Street Gang, *Webster*   187
Streets of Laredo, The, *American ballad*   28
Swagless Swaggie, The, *Harrington*   148

Tarpauling Jacket, *Anonymous*   64
Three Butchers, The, *Anonymous*   102
Troubadour, The, *Gilbert*   75
Tying a Knot in the Devil's Tail, *Anonymous*   35

Village Burglar, The, *Anonymous*   227

Whisky Bill, *American cowboy ballad*   13
Wild Colonial Boy, The, *Australian folk ballad*   171
Wolves, The, *Kinnell*   95

Acknowledgments (continued from copyright page)

Dorothy Howard, for her poem "The Knifesmith," which first appeared in *The Poetry Review.*

J. B. Lippincott Co., for "Saint George and the Dragon" from *A Letter to Lucian and Other Poems* by Alfred Noyes. Published in the United States in 1957 by J. B. Lippincott Company.

The Macmillan Company, for "The Man He Killed" from *Collected Poems* by Thomas Hardy, copyright 1925 by The Macmillan Company; for "Daniel" from *Collected Poems* by Vachel Lindsay, copyright 1920 by The Macmillan Company, renewed 1948 by Elizabeth C. Lindsay; and for "Seumas Beg" from *Collected Poems* by James Stephens, copyright 1929 by The Macmillan Company, renewed 1937 by James Stephens. All reprinted by permission of The Macmillan Company.

Macmillan & Co. Ltd., London, for "The Messages" by Michael Gibson.

Christopher Mann Ltd., London, for "The Song of the Banana Man" by Evan Jones. First published by "Bim," Bridgetown, Barbados, in 1952.

Julian Mitchell, for his poem "Lament for the Cowboy Life."

Poetry Magazine, for "Proud Riders" by H. L. Davis.

New Directions Publishing Corp., for "Dulce et Decorum Est" from *Collected Poems* by Wilfred Owen, copyright Chatto & Windus, Ltd., 1946, © 1963. Reprinted by permission of New Directions Publishing Corporation.

Random House, Inc., for "Spanish Johnny" from *April Twilights* by Willa Cather, copyright 1923 and renewed 1951 by The Executors of the Estate of Willa Cather, reprinted by permission of Alfred A. Knopf, Inc.; and "Danny" by John M. Synge, copyright 1909 and renewed 1936 by Edward Synge and Francis Edmund Stephens, reprinted from *The Complete Works of John M. Synge* by permission of Random House, Inc.

Ben Roth Agency, Inc., for "Mules" by G. Fox Smith, copyright © Punch Publications, London.

Martha Keller Rowland, for "Andrew Jackson" from *Brady's Bend* by Martha Keller, copyright 1946 by Martha Keller Rowland, published by Rutgers University Press.

Vernon Scannell, for his poems "Mastering the Craft," "Peerless Jim Driscoll," "A Kind of Hero," and "First Fight." "Mastering the Craft" first appeared in *Encounter* Magazine.

Scott, Foresman and Company for "Rodeo" by Edward Lueders from *Reflections on a Gift of Watermelon Pickle and Other Modern Verse* by Stephen Dunning, Edward Lueders, and Hugh Smith, copyright © 1966 by Scott, Foresman and Company.

Charles Scribner's Sons, Publishers, for "Juan Belmonte, Torero," reprinted with the permission of Charles Scribner's Sons from *The Clothing's New Emperor and Other Poems* by Donald Finkel, copyright © 1959 by Donald Finkel (*Poets of Today VI*); and for "Reuben Bright" from *Children of the Night* by Edward Arlington Robinson, published by Charles Scribner's Sons.

Sheed and Ward, Inc., Publishers, for "Boxer" by Joseph P. Clancy. From *Beginnings,* © 1956 Sheed and Ward, Inc., New York.

Shel Silverstein, for his poem "The Hunter."

The University of Chicago Press, for " 'Plot Improbable, Character Unsympathetic' " from *Plays and Poems* by Elder Olson, copyright © 1958 by The University of Chicago, published 1958.

Louis Untermeyer, for his translation of "Ballade" by Edmond Rostand. First published in his translation of Rostand's *Cyrano de Bergerac* issued by The Limited Editions Club, 1954. Copyright 1954 by Louis Untermeyer.

The Viking Press, Inc., for "Counter-Attack" from *Collected Poems* by Siegfried Sassoon, copyright 1918 by E. P. Dutton & Co., renewed 1946 by Siegfried Sassoon; and for "The Hero" from *Collected Poems* by Siegfried Sassoon, copyright 1918 by E. P. Dutton & Co. All rights reserved. Both reprinted by permission of The Viking Press, Inc.

H. Webster, for his poem "Street Gang."

Wesleyan University Press, for "Carentan O Carentan," copyright © 1959 by Louis Simpson. Reprinted from *A Dream of Governors* by Louis Simpson by permission of Wesleyan University Press.

7942